U-BOAT
WARFARE

THE EVOLUTION
OF THE WOLF PACK

U-BOAT
WARFARE

THE EVOLUTION
OF THE WOLF PACK

Jak P. Mallmann Showell

Ian Allan
60th
ANNIVERSARY

First published 2002

ISBN 0 7110 2887 7

Published by Ian Allan Publishing

an imprint of Ian Allan Publishing Ltd, Hersham, Surrey KT12 4RG.
Printed by Ian Allan Printing Ltd, Hersham, Surrey KT12 4RG.

Code: 0208/A2

Front cover:
This probably shows *U66* (ObLtzS Gerhard Seehausen) sinking. It was an ocean-going boat of Type IXC used for long-range operations to America and into the South Atlantic. See page 79 for additional details.

Back cover:
Refueling at sea. It was standard practice to refuel with one ship being towed behind another, rather than sailing side by side. See Chapter 12 for additional details.

Half title page:
German torpedoes could be adjusted to detonate magnetically when passing under the target or by contact when colliding with the side. See page 21 for additional details.

Title page:
This photograph was probably taken from *U47* under KptIt Günther Prien, who torpedoed the battleship HMS *Royal Oak* inside the naval anchorage at Scapa Flow. It shows men from a stopped merchant ship coming alongside with a briefcase containing their ship's papers. See page 14 for additional details.

Contents

Introduction

This book is based on the U-boat Command's war diary, which has become known under a variety of different names, but was the log book kept by Admiral Karl Dönitz and his staff, known in German as the *Kriegstagebuch des Befehlshaber der Unterseeboote-Operationen* (KTB des BdU-Ops). These A4 typed pages occupy enough shelf space to make a detailed study rather daunting. However, immediately after the war Dönitz's son-in-law (the ex-U-boat commander and U-boat Command staff officer, Günter Hessler) led a German team to collaborate with the Allies in compiling a detailed history of the war at sea. This has recently been published anonymously by HMSO under the title of *The U-boat War in the Atlantic 1939–1945* and provides a fascinating condensed guide to this vast diary.

The rest of the information has come mainly from documents in the International Submarine Archive (*U-Boot-Archiv*) in Cuxhaven-Altenbruch (Germany) and I should like to thank Horst Bredow and Horst Schwenk for helping me gain access to those papers. In addition to this, I should like to express my thanks to all those who have helped in supporting the archive to become the leading source for information about U-boats.

Information from the Allied side has come mainly from two important sources: first, unpublished documents from the library of the Royal Navy Submarine Museum (HMS *Dolphin*) at Gosport, in connection with which I should like to thank Margaret Bidmead for her great support; and, secondly, unpublished material kept in the archive at Bletchley Park, in connection with which I should like to thank the senior archivist, John Gallehawk, for helping me struggle through the papers. Although many of the documents from these two centres are also available at the Public Record Office, both the Submarine Museum and Bletchley Park provided considerable help and encouragement in understanding this somewhat overwhelming material. In truth, many of the facts and figures are useless unless there is a helping hand available to translate the raw data into manageable bites.

I am also most grateful to all the people who have helped me in the past, many of whom have been mentioned in the text or in previous books. However, I must apologise for forgetting until now to acknowledge the help and inspiration from Michael Cooper and Roger Suiters. I should also like to thank the many members of FTU (Friends of Traditionsarchiv Unterseeboote) who have helped with the research. I am grateful to Bill Love, a World War 2 fighter pilot from the RAF, for checking the manuscript before it went to print.

Although every effort is made to eliminate mistakes, a few gremlins always seem to get through and I should like to thank all the people who have drawn my attention to irregularities arising in the past. I am especially grateful to those who have taken the trouble to illuminate the more obscure topics.

Pictures

Photographs have come from *U-Boot-Archiv*, 27478 Cuxhaven-Altenbruch (Germany) or from the author's collection. The maps were first printed in the author's book *U-boat Command and the Battle of the Atlantic*.

Above: U203 (Kptlt Rolf Mützelburg) being towed out to sea on its first trials in February 1941. In circumstances like these the ice could damage the propellers, therefore submarines were towed into the open sea before casting off to continue under their own steam.

Chapter 1

The Battle of the Atlantic

The debate about who was first to come up with the U-boat wolf pack concept has generated so much steam that the majority of participants have failed to notice that grazing animals gain considerable advantages by wandering around in herds and, since the beginning of time, successful carnivores have known that they stood a better chance of gaining a meal if they pursued these herds with organised groups, rather than individuals going it alone. Even man, when he appeared on the scene thousands of years later, was quick to discover that mammoth steaks were easier to acquire when working with a team instead of challenging his lunch on the hoof with just one spear.

During World War 1 U-boats were partly defeated by sailing merchant ships in convoys which were protected by small, fast warships. This battle came to an end before U-boat group attacks could be organised in earnest, but it was not too difficult to predict that this was likely to be the next step. To make an impact upon a convoy, it was advisable to attack with well co-ordinated groups. The trouble with this theory is that there is a considerable difference between thinking it out from the luxury of an armchair and applying the principle over the vastness of a restless ocean.

In 1935, when Fregattenkapitän (Fregkpt) Karl Dönitz commissioned Germany's new U-boat flotilla, the initial objective was to get the men acquainted with their new weapons and, therefore, the first major wargame did not take place until the autumn of 1938, when the light cruiser *Königsberg* served as floating headquarters for the U-boat staff. This exercise was a terrific success. A mock-up convoy, protected by anti-submarine hunters, was 'decimated', and the small boats for retrieving spent torpedoes worked overtime. Lights made good peacetime weapons. Fitted in the warheads of practice torpedoes, they allowed observers to gain an intriguing picture in the blackness of the night. The U-boat staff had good reasons for their high spirits. Those few days of dummy war showed that the wolf pack tactic offered excellent prospects.

However, not everyone shared the enthusiasm. Among the sceptics was Otto Köhler, a young lieutenant of 29, who had come into the navy straight from university and had been selected as liaison officer between the ship's company and the U-boat staff. He pointed out that the wargame would almost certainly have ended differently had the new invention of radar been switched on. After all, this electronic device made it possible for the *Königsberg* to slip in and out of harbour during the thickest fogs because it showed up obstructions in the deep water channel. Therefore, it should also be capable of seeing U-boats during the darkest of nights.

The German naval leadership, however, showed no great enthusiasm for this invention. It was thought to be too detrimental for the small navy, whose main advantage was to remain hidden from potential attackers. Radar signals travelled considerably longer distances than those at which targets could be detected. Therefore, it was possible for an enemy to discover the presence of a radar set without the owners being aware that an eavesdropper was watching their every move. In view of this great disadvantage, Germany developed the system as an additional aid for ranging guns during bad weather after the target had been visually sighted, rather than as a detection device.

Above: The coat being worn by the officer on the left may suggest this is winter, but the piston rings on his sleeve indicate that this is not a greatcoat but the rarer frock coat worn only for official functions. The date is 6 August 1938 and this small piece of history shows the commissioning of *U51* (Type VIIB) in the naval dockyard in Kiel. (That rather characteristic building behind the left flagpole was still standing at the end of the century.) The picture is of special interest because it shows how little thought had been given to defence against aircraft. The one small 20mm anti-aircraft gun had not yet found a place on the top of the conning tower. Instead it was accommodated on the upper deck, just aft of the tower, where waves often made it impossible to use. The general consensus of opinion at this time was that submarines would dive long before an aircraft came close enough to be troublesome.

One major snag with radar was that only a few people understood its intricacies and in the early days the delicate equipment was usually installed on top of a gun turret, where it received a considerable battering every time a salvo was fired. Consequently it quickly gave up the ghost and several valves had to be replaced before it could be got to work again. This weakness was exploited by die-hard conventionalists to emphasise the advantages of optical range finders. Dönitz apparently did not even take the trouble to examine the equipment, so it is likely that he had been influenced by the negative gossip. Possibly his mind was also filled with a far more intimidating threat: that of the underwater sound detector.

Very little was known about it at the time, other than that British anti-submarine experts put great faith in the 'pinger' for detecting submerged submarines. Called asdic, after the Allied Submarine Detection Investigation Committee, it was said to render submarine attacks virtually impossible by locating them as they approached below the waves.

The Supreme Naval Command did not share the U-boat staff's enthusiasm for group attacks. Even Dönitz himself was still not fully convinced and was quick to admit that there were many unsolved problems, but he felt that wolf packs offered the best chances of success. Despite this, they did not feature in the navy's war plans and mobilisation schedules were not modified to accommodate this newly introduced concept. The emergency war plans, devised by the Supreme Naval Command and put into effect during the middle of August 1939, dictated that U-boats should be positioned around the British Isles to operate on their own without support and without opportunities to co-operate. Therefore, after the outbreak of war, considerable backstage manoeuvring was necessary before boats could be recalled and the first wolf pack organised. Yet, despite concerted attempts to launch such attacks, the efforts were continuously frustrated by one gremlin after another and a year was to pass before a U-boat group brought any significant success.

Hitler's orders also limited U-boat operations at first by insisting that they work within the internationally agreed Prize Ordinance regulations. These regulations demanded that merchant ships should be stopped and papers be inspected before any aggressive action was taken, whether the attacker was a surface warship or a submarine. Even then, the target was allowed to be sunk only if it was carrying contraband, and not

Above: U26 (Type IA) was commissioned on 11 May 1936, without anti-aircraft armament. The inscription on the horseshoe-shaped lifebelt, hanging on the side of the tower, says '*Flotilla Saltzwedel*'. This flotilla shared a depot and facilities with Flotilla *Hundius* in Wilhelmshaven, which was due to have formed the first wolf pack of World War 2. The numbers on the side of the conning tower were removed once the war started.

until the submariners had seen to the safety of the crew — and putting them into their lifeboats in the middle of the ocean was not enough. This was a virtually impossible hurdle when it came to the practicalities of submarine warfare. The space inside U-boats was so cramped that there was simply no space for additional bodies like enemy merchant ship crews. By contrast, convoys presented good opportunities for U-boats because they came within a category of shipping which could be attacked without warning.

Despite these difficulties, Hitler insisted that the last of the limiting regulations should remain in force for the best part of a year, until August 1940, but even then no great number of wolf packs were formed simply because there were not enough boats to form patrol lines. However, group attacks, where a number of U-boats converged on the same convoy, resulted in sinking figures rising out of all proportions. The important point about this so-called 'Happy Time' was that the staggering successes were not so much due to groups of U-boats converging on the same convoy, but to the tactic of short-range, surface attack at night. This concept was formulated by U-boat commanders themselves and launched without a great deal of guidance from Karl Dönitz. So far, the expected practice had been to attack from a range of several kilometres by firing a salvo of two or more torpedoes from a submerged position.

However, U-boat commanders found that it was possible to approach convoys on the surface at night and to attack from such short range that they could almost guarantee a hit with a single torpedo. The results were so devastating that some historians have claimed U-boats almost came within reach of winning the Battle of the Atlantic, yet they failed to explain how such a small number of submarines, often fewer than a dozen at sea, could defeat the most powerful navy on earth. Never mind, propaganda is always stronger than the truth.

The state of affairs in the Atlantic changed rapidly during the spring of 1941. The sinking of a number of U-boat aces in March marked the beginning of a difficult period when German submarines hardly came within range to fire torpedoes. This was made worse in May, when code books and an Enigma machine were captured from Kapitänleutnant (Kptlt) Fritz-Julius Lemp's *U110* and the British code-breakers at Bletchley Park gained an insight into the principal German naval code. Being virtually one step ahead all the time, the British convoy controllers avoided pack after pack, while the German leaders twisted and turned under an onslaught of frustration. Dönitz was forced constantly to modify the wolf pack principle. In this period different ways of forming patrol lines were tried out in earnest and the true wolf pack attack, rather than the group attack, started to take shape. The main problem was that the majority of U-boats failed to find

convoys and only a small fraction of the total actually came close enough to launch torpedoes.

Most of the action during the autumn of 1940 had taken place in the Western Approaches, where the convoy routes funnelled towards the comparatively narrow space between Northern Ireland and Great Britain. In 1941, the U-boats were driven further west, where the difficulty was more one of finding convoys rather than attacking them, and various theories about the formation of patrol lines were put to the test. The discussion ranged basically between whether boats should sail backwards and forwards one behind the other at right angles to an approaching convoy or whether it might be better to sail parallel to the merchant ships. The first idea was quickly abandoned because it offered too many opportunities for convoys to slip through the patrol line without being spotted. U-boats were so far apart that they could not see each other and the turning times for the backward and forward movements would have been impossible to co-ordinate. There were far too many opportunities for two boats in the chain to be travelling away from each other while a convoy slipped through the gap. Even with the patrol line sailing on a parallel course to the expected convoy, there were still mountains of opportunities for gaps to become so big that merchant ships could slip through. One of the biggest problems was navigating

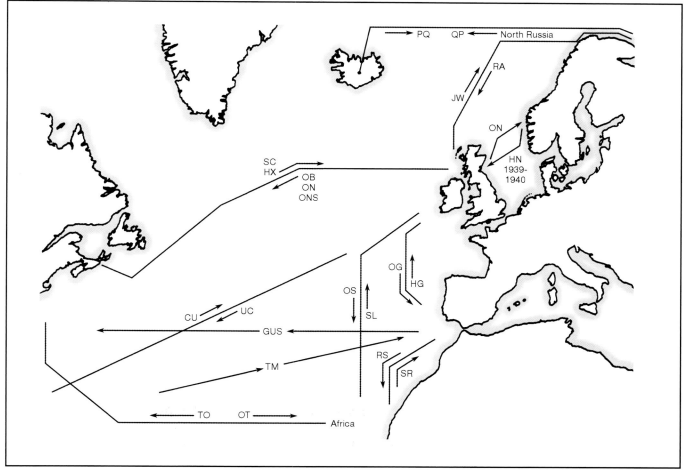

Above: The major North Atlantic convoy routes. CU=Caribbean–UK; GUS=Gibraltar–North America; HN=Norway–UK; HG=Gibraltar–UK; JW=Scotland–North Russia; OB=UK–North America; OG=UK–Gibraltar; ON=UK–Norway (later UK–North America); ONS=UK–North America (slow); OS=UK–West Africa; OT=America–Africa; PQ=Iceland–North Russia; QP= North Russia–Iceland; RA=North Russia–Scotland; RS–Gibraltar–West Africa; SC=Halifax–UK; SL=Sierra Leone–UK; SR=West Africa–Gibraltar; TM=Trinidad–Gibraltar; TO=Africa–America; UC=UK–Caribbean. (The suffix 'S' indicated a slow convoy.)

Above: Otto Köhler challenged Dönitz's concept of the wolf pack attack, but later became a U-boat Commander. After his release from Spandau prison, Dönitz said that he could not remember this difference of opinion with Köhler, but Claus Korth (commander of *U57* and *U93* and later Third Staff Officer with the U-boat arm's Organisation Department) told the author in the late 1970s that it must have been quite a verbal brawl because he remembered hearing about it and he had not been present at the heated discussion.

on exceedingly restless water when both sun and stars could be obscured for days on end, making it virtually impossible to determine accurate positions.

None of the German efforts paid dividends, but the lack of success was quickly forgotten during the first months of 1942, when U-boats attacked shipping off the eastern seaboard of the United States. There Germany found an abundance of easy targets because various reasons prevented America from declaring a state of emergency and very little effort was made to fight back. Consequently, the bloody bonanza which followed became known as the U-boats' 'Second Golden Time' or 'Second Happy Time'. Targets came so fast that there was never time to form wolf packs and U-boats operated with virtual immunity until the summer of 1942, when aggressive retaliation forced them away from the coast, back into the remains of the air gap (the area not covered by Allied land-based air reconnaissance) of the central Atlantic. Once again wolf packs

were formed to hunt elusive convoys, but despite a period of nine months when Bletchley Park was unable to read the principal German code, British experts still managed to route many convoys around the U-boat patrol lines. (This blackout started in February 1942, when Atlantic U-boats changed to a new four-wheel Enigma machine, and remained in force until December after one of these devices, together with its code books, was captured in November from *U559* (Kptlt Hans Heidtmann) by men from HMS *Petard*.)

The exceptionally harsh continental winter of 1941–2 had resulted in the Baltic remaining frozen until late in the year, preventing the training of new U-boat crews. However, the construction yards continued working, meaning that the summer of 1942 saw an unusually large number of boats waiting to be unleashed on the shipping lanes of the North Atlantic. The total number of boats at sea started rising from spring 1942 onwards. In June there were almost 60 boats at sea, in July it was 70, in August 86 and by September it reached a staggering 100, and it remained at that high number until May of the following year. Of course, the figure of 100 U-boats at sea included those on their way out and on their way home, therefore the number available for forming a wolf pack was usually only about one third of the total. This still meant that there was sufficient hitting power in the form of torpedoes at sea to have the potential for sinking well over 1,000 ships per month.

Obviously, such large numbers of U-boats at sea meant that their successes were impressively high and the British propaganda system tightened the thumbscrews even further by suggesting Britain was on the brink of a disastrous defeat to ensure production lines were kept rolling. Yet, despite the Enigma blackout, the Allies must have known that the majority of U-boats never came within shooting range of a target. This state of affairs was staggering. In 1940, during the 'Happy Time', every U-boat at sea was sinking almost six merchant ships per month. Now, two years later, in autumn 1942, that figure had dropped to less than one and at times sank as low as one-half. In other words, two U-boats were required at sea every month to sink one merchant ship. This meant that the Allied, or rather the British, anti-submarine efforts had already made a significant impact, despite that important blackout at Bletchley Park.

That high number of about 100 U-boats at sea per day meant that a clash of gigantic proportions was inevitable. In March 1943, the fast convoy HX229 was in the process of merging with the slower SC122 when almost 100 merchant ships came into contact with a huge wolf pack. Inadequate escorts were stretched to the limit and the results were devastating. Yet, by this time Britain had gained access to Germany's new radio code and the turnaround of events was even more dramatic. A couple of weeks later, convoy HX231 with Escort Group B7 under Commander Peter Gretton reached Britain having lost only six ships and thrown off almost all attacking U-boats.

The battle for convoys HX229 and SC122 has often been described as a major turning point in the Battle of the Atlantic. Yet, the fact that such a massive battle took place only in March 1943 is highly significant. A very important question, which has never been answered, is why had that action not taken place during the preceding six months? After all, Germany had had 100 U-boats at sea since the summer of the preceding year. This shows that the British anti-submarine measures had already made a significant impact and that the role of Britain breaking into the Enigma code has often been overestimated.

Despite the momentous actions of March 1943, the number of U-boats sunk did not rise dramatically until May.

The U-boat losses for this period, when there were about 100 U-boats at sea, are as follows:

MONTH	NUMBER OF U–BOATS LOST
1942	
August	10
September	11
October	16
November	13
December	5
1943	
January	6
February	19
March	16
April	15
May	42
June	17
July	39

U-boat losses have been overshadowed by the disastrous Black May of 1943 to such an extent that many historians have ignored the fact that the sinkings leading up to that month were also incredibly high. One needs to bear in mind that the figures in the above table add up to a loss approaching almost a thousand men per month. On top of that, the resources necessary to get those men to sea were enormous. In May, when that figure rose to over 40, Admiral Dönitz moved boats out of the shipping lanes of the North Atlantic into what he thought were safer areas. Many historians have referred to this as the 'turning point' in the war, yet Dönitz did not look upon it as such at the time. For him it was a temporary withdrawal until new weapons could be brought into service.

The modification of removing the large deck gun in front of the conning tower and strengthening the anti-aircraft armament had already started during 1942 and new acoustic torpedoes, for use against fast, shallow draught warships, were due to come into service towards the end of 1943. There were also new anti-convoy torpedoes, an array of technical installations for detecting enemy radar and, on top of this, boats were being equipped with radar foxers. So the prospects looked promising. The U-boat Command was convinced that it was only a matter of time before fortunes would change in the German favour. Amidst the gloom of heavy losses during the summer of 1943, and horrific bombing attacks against civilians in German cities, came the news that much of this latest gear was going to be available well ahead of schedule. Consequently the autumn of 1943 saw a dramatic resumption of the convoy war in the shipping lanes of the North Atlantic. The results were devastating, but not for the Allies. The attacking wolf packs were cut to shreds and the year ended on a firmly depressing note for the U-boats. To many it was clear that U-boats could no longer operate against the powerful opposition in the North Atlantic.

Despite this distressing situation, not all was lost. New types of submarines were already lying on the slips and Dönitz hoped that it was only a matter of time before they would be in a position to regain the upper hand. The new Type XXI was faster

under water than the majority of escorts on the surface. So, once more, the prospects looked good. The snag was that at it would be least nine months before the new boats could be expected to make an appearance. In the meantime Dönitz felt that Germany could not abandon the war at sea. Therefore, U-boats were continuously sent on operations, a high proportion of them with inexperienced crews, who had received only the barest of rudimentary training, and many never returned. Indeed a vast number were lost during their first operational voyage. Germany struggled on, but sadly could contribute only towards its own losses.

The losses and the successes are indeed staggering and historians, together with Allied propaganda, have projected a somewhat misleading image of what actually happened. For example, many historians have told us that some 1,160 merchant ships were sunk by U-boats during 1942, but they have failed to say that the natural wastage of ships lost due to collision, stranding, fire and foundering added up to 432. In addition to this, the by-now famous cliché of Britain being faced by over a thousand U-boats hardly bears examination. Germany did commission 1,171 submarines but their involvement in the war shows a different picture.

U–BOAT INVOLVEMENT IN THE WAR AT SEA WAS AS FOLLOWS		
38	U-boats attacked and at least damaged	20 or more ships
45	U-boats attacked and at least damaged	11–19 ships.
72	U-boats attacked and at least damaged	6–10 ships.
307	U-boats attacked and at least damaged	1–5 ships.
674	U-boats never hit a target at all.	

This adds up to 1,136 so there are a few unaccounted boats and some, such as supply submarines and experimental craft, were never in a position to attack shipping, but one is still left with a staggering total of well over 600 boats which contributed only to Germany's losses, without hitting at the all-important trade routes. Incidentally, the discrepancy between these figures and those in my previous book *U-boats under the Swastika* is due to the numbers above being based on Peter Sharpe's *U-boat Fact File*, which covers all sea areas, whereas the analysis in *U-boats under the Swastika* deals with only the Battle of the Atlantic.

When one looks at the battle from the human point of view, one sees an even more startling picture. A total of 2,450 ships was sunk in the Atlantic by U-boats and this figure climbs to 2,775 when one adds the sinkings in other sea areas. Of these, 800 were sent to the bottom by 30 U-boat commanders. In other words, 2% of the commanders were responsible for destroying 30% of all Allied shipping. This shows that the teeth of those wolf packs were indeed owned by a tiny fraction of the total. It may be interesting to add that 1,207 merchant ships and 158 warships were sent to the bottom of the Atlantic by firing a single torpedo. However, 5,157 merchant ships and 786 warships were actually attacked in that theatre, showing that there was a considerable failure rate.

To calculate the maximum number of ships which could have been sunk throughout the war is rather difficult, but the following gives some indication of the number of voyages undertaken.

NO. OF VOYAGES	NO. OF U–BOATS
0 (never sailed on an operational voyage)	293
1	262
2	150
3	101
4	60
5	54
6	30
7	32
8	30
9	27
10	37
11	16
12	12
13–22	29

Again, these figures fall short of the total number commissioned, but give some indication of the futility of devoting so much money and so many resources to the building of submarines.

After the war, the Royal Navy calculated that the average number of torpedoes carried was 13, so therefore these voyages allow for over 40,000 torpedoes to have been carried into action. Not all of those voyages would have pitched U-boats against shipping, and it is exceedingly difficult to come up with a realistic figure. Yet, this does seem to show that the total destruction potential of the U-boat Arm surpassed by far the actual numbers sunk.

The first U-boat groups were small and the period of time between dissolving one and forming another so great that a means of identification was hardly necessary. Convoys were merely identified with the name of the first U-boat to have sighted them. Later, packs were given names, often dramatic ones from history or legend. However, not all of these were wolf packs in the true sense. Boats sailing to the Far East and operating in the Indian Ocean before returning as cargo carriers were known as *Monsun* boats. They hardly met at sea, except for refuelling or in emergencies, and operated as independent units without communicating with each other. Another example is the *Eisbär* group, which sailed to South Africa, but whose members operated more or less as independent boats without too much communication between them. Often these special undertakings are easier to identify because the word 'Operation' preceded the name: Operation *Paukenschlag*, the first attack against the United States; Operation *Pastorius*, the landing of agents in America; Operation *Taube*, landing agents in Ireland and so on.

Wolf packs were rather fluid formations and they must not be looked upon as a solid group such as escort flotillas or other military units. The boats themselves had no connection with one another, often coming from different bases, and packs were usually formed while the majority of individuals were already at

sea. Therefore, it is highly unlikely that all the commanders would have known each other personally, in the way one member of an air force squadron knew another. In addition to this, some boats were assigned to packs after they had been sunk, but the U-boat Command was not yet aware of the demise. Some U-boats didn't pick up the radio call to join a pack and therefore did not join the patrol line. There were navigational problems, especially during poor weather when the sun and stars were obscured for days on end, making it impossible to find the patrol line. On other occasions the U-boat Command ordered boats to proceed at fast cruising speed of about 12 knots, but the winds were so appalling that boats could manage only five. Some boats were a considerable distance from where U-boat Command thought they should be and did not reach the patrol line on time. The number of gremlins were virtually endless, yet despite all these problems, a good number of successfully tight patrol lines were formed.

Finally, as far as terminology is concerned, the term 'wolf pack' was hardly used throughout the war, the U-boat Command tending to refer to each group as a 'patrol line' or 'reconnaissance line'.

Above: The long and slender lines of a Type VIIC, probably *U564* under Kptlt Reinhard Suhren, with the larger 'Wintergarten' or conservatory extension at the aft end of the conning tower. The partly raised attack periscope can be seen towards the middle of the conning tower, while the extendable rod aerial can also be seen towards the right.

Left:
Although strong sunlight has produced a stark shadow over his eyes, this does show one of those typical images of Dönitz. Once a junior officer had the courage to ask him why he went around with his coat unbuttoned. Regulations stated that greatcoats had to be buttoned up to the neck, except for admirals who wore the lapels open to reveal the cornflower blue lining. Dönitz wasn't perturbed by the rather brash question and answered saying that he looked too insignificant among the crowds and had to do something to make people take note that he was the boss. Therefore, when there were no higher ranks around, he did not follow the regulations about buttoning his coat.

Right:
Karl Dönitz, the Supreme Commander-in-Chief for U-boats as Vizeadmiral, seen here visiting the 7th U-Flotilla in St Nazaire (France) with flotilla leader, Korvkpt Herbert Sohler, on the left.

Above: U37 being supplied in Lorient. This large ocean-going Type IX shows how the conning tower has been modified to protect lookouts from spray, waves and wind by having two lips added to the front. The flange halfway up the tower was called the 'spray deflector', while the 'wind deflector' was at the top edge. Although this was the biggest type of U-boat when it was commissioned, the conning tower still had only a small gun platform or Wintergarten with one single 20mm anti-aircraft gun.

Right: This photograph was probably taken from *U47* under Kptlt Günther Prien, who torpedoed the battleship HMS *Royal Oak* inside the naval anchorage at Scapa Flow. It shows men from a stopped merchant ship coming alongside with a briefcase containing their ship's papers. At the beginning of the war U-boats were restricted by Prize Ordinance regulations, which stated that ship's papers had to be inspected. The target could be sunk only if it was carrying goods included in the contraband list.

Chapter 2

The War Starts September 1939–April 1940

During the middle of August 1939, when the U-boat Chief (Kapitän zur See und Kommodore Karl Dönitz) was on leave in southern Germany, the Supreme Naval Command in Berlin ordered the 'Three Front War Programme' to be put into immediate effect. This state of emergency prepared for a possible war in the Baltic, North Sea and Atlantic, and stipulated that naval units should be positioned in independent operational areas on the high seas to prevent them being cut off in ports by superior blockading forces. The plan ran relatively smoothly, although the U-boat leadership found stumbling through a mass of code words rather confusing, but despite this, the majority of submarines had reached their secret positions by the time Britain and France declared war on 3 September 1939. By then, it was also obvious that there would be no need for U-boats in the Baltic and therefore Dönitz quickly moved his headquarters to Sengwarden near Wilhelmshaven. Some historians have stated that the harbour there soon became a bustling U-boat base, which is rather absurd since the isolated wooden huts were several kilometres inland and the only water was a narrow ditch, draining the low-lying pastures. Although it took a good while, along bumpy cobblestone roads, to reach the spot from the naval base, there were good telephone connections and Dönitz quickly asked the Supreme Naval Command for permission to bring the U-boats home. His argument was that the British authorities would have removed vulnerable merchant shipping from the sea lanes before declaring war. In view of this, he suggested it would be better to have the boats fully fuelled and provisioned when this traffic re-emerged from its safe havens. Intelligence suggested that Weymouth, on England's south

coast, was likely to be a major emergency wartime port and Dönitz thought that shipping running to or from Gibraltar would make the best target. Therefore plans were made to intercept this with a wolf pack.

No one knew who should command such a pack, where this key person should be located, how U-boats might be called together, or whether such action was at all possible over the vastness of the Atlantic. Radio, after all, was still very much in its infancy and many German sailors tended to shy away from using it because they feared their position would be determined by British radio direction finders. To overcome this, the Kriegsmarine introduced a special Short Signal Code Book, with which it was possible to send quite lengthy information by transmitting just a few letters of Morse code. It was thought that these special transmissions were too brief for radio direction finders to get a bearing on them. This fear of radio direction finders was one of the decisive factors in favour of establishing a land-based control centre. The naval version of the Enigma coding machine was considered 'unbreakable' and therefore it was thought that there would be no danger in sending lengthy messages from a known site. Should the British capture a machine set up with the code of the day, it would only be possible to read signals until the settings were changed for the next 24 hours. There

Below: The naval barracks at Bant in Wilhelmshaven, home for two U-boat flotillas, seen here during the calm days before the outbreak of war, with *U30*, *U28* and *U29* in the foreground. These boats belonged to the 2nd or *Saltzwedel* Flotilla and shared the facilities with the 6th or *Hundius* Flotilla, which was due to have formed the first wolf pack. In the event, there were too few boats at sea and the plan fell flat.

were so many variations in settings that every book in Germany could be passed through an Enigma machine without repeating the same setting.

Prewar exercises had been played out over considerably smaller distances than Atlantic dimensions, and rehearsals concentrated more on the attack rather than the assembling of wolf packs, meaning that the U-boat leadership was indeed faced with a number of complicated conundrums. Choosing a pack leader was overcome by replacing the captain of *U37* (Kptlt Heinrich Schuch) with Korvettenkapitän (Korvkpt) Werner Hartmann, the commander of the 6th U-boat Flotilla (Flotilla *Hundius*) in Wilhelmshaven. It was thought that he would be in the best position to command both the boat and the wolf pack out in the Atlantic. The plan was to bring the group together around the south of Ireland and then sweep past the Bay of Biscay towards Gibraltar. *U37* was chosen because it was a large ocean-going Type IXA with special facilities, in particular an unusually large number of radios, for the flotilla leader's small staff. The passage through the English Channel was considered to be too dangerous for such a large group so the boats were routed from Kiel and Wilhelmshaven around the north of Scotland.

During these early stages, it was intended that the first wolf pack should be made up as follows:

BOAT	COMMANDER	PORT AND DATE SAILED
U37	Werner Hartmann	Wilhelmshaven on 5 October 1939
U25	Viktor Schütze	Wilhelmshaven on 18 October
U34	Wilhelm Rollmann	Wilhelmshaven on 17 October
U40	Wolfgang Barten	Wilhelmshaven on 10 October
U42	Rolf Dau	Wilhelmshaven on 2 October
U45	Alexander Gelhaar	Kiel on 5 October
U46	Herbert Sohler	Kiel on 6 October
U47	Günther Prien	Withdrawn before sailing
U48	Herbert Schultze	Kiel on 10 October

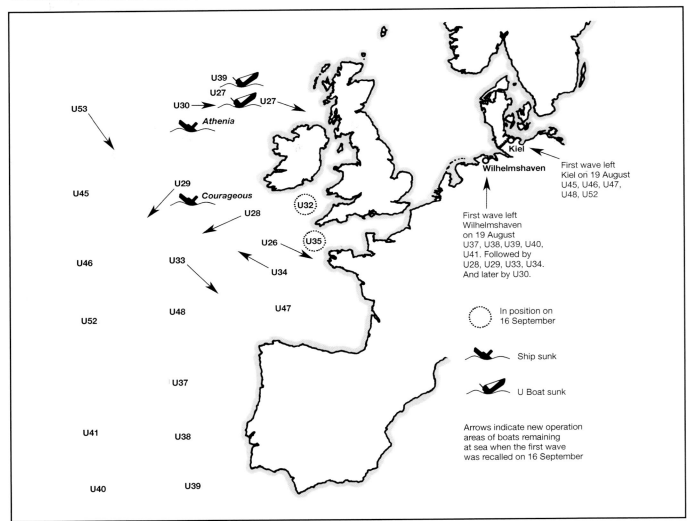

Above: U-boat positions on 6 September 1939. The U-boat commanders were: *U26* Fregkpt Oskar Schomburg; *U27* Kptlt Johannes Franz; *U28* Kptlt Günter Kuhnke; *U29* Kptlt Otto Schuhart; *U30* Kptlt Fritz-Julius Lemp; *U32* ObltzS Hans Jenisch; *U33* Kptlt Hans-Wilhelm von Dresky; *U34* Kptlt Wilhelm Rollmann; *U35* Kptlt Werner Lot; *U37* Kptlt Heinrich Schuch; *U38* Kptlt Heinrich Liebe; *U40* Kptlt Werner von Schmidt; *U41* Kptlt Gustav-Adolf Mugler; *U45* Kptlt Alexander Gelhaar; *U46* Kptlt Herbert Sohler; *U47* Kptlt Günther Prien; *U48* Kptlt Herbert Schultze; *U52* Kptlt Wolfgang Barten; *U53* Kptlt Ernst-Günther Heinicke.

Instead of joining the pack, U47 was selected for the special mission to penetrate into the Royal Navy's anchorage at Scapa Flow, where the battleship *Royal Oak* was sunk. U25 and U34 remained in dock for repairs and did not leave until it was too late. U40, U42 and U45 were sunk en route, thus leaving the potential pack rather short. As things turned out, the situation at sea was somewhat different from what Dönitz had expected. The majority of merchant ships had not been drawn together in convoys and U-boats encountered a good number of independents, which had to be stopped according to Prize Ordinance regulations. The rest of the autumn continued in a similar vein, with a shortage of boats making it impractical to assemble wolf packs.

Half a year of war was to pass before an officer at sea, rather than the Operations Room on land, was unexpectedly to be in a position possibly to form the first wolf pack. This happened in February 1940, when Kptlt Herbert Schultze in U48 found himself faced with a convoy and the knowledge that there were several other boats in the near vicinity. Frustration set in rather quickly when he realised that he was not carrying the same charts nor the same radio code as other boats, meaning he could not communicate directly, and it was too late by the time the sighting had been relayed by the land-based operations room. The reason for the difference in charts and codes was due to U48 having been sent on an especially dangerous mission to mine Weymouth harbour, where there was a high risk of being disabled in shallow water and hence of Britain gaining access to the Enigma coding machine, code books and the secret naval charts. Consequently, the prospects of setting up the first wolf pack of the war fell flat.

This was not looked upon as being detrimental and Herbert Schultze wrote a most favourable report on the first few months of the war. He told Dönitz that the performance of the boat and crew was considerably better than expected from earlier exercises. Experience had shown the pressure hull to be excellent and only a few minor problems had occurred. The torpedo tubes worked well, but the attack periscope had such limited use that submerged attacks were virtually out of the question. Both the magnification and the clarity, especially towards the rim, were nowhere near good enough. Condensation on the optics inside the tube presented far too great a problem. In fact, one attack had to be aborted because it was impossible to see the target. This occurred when a newcomer, who had transferred from another boat, automatically followed earlier standing instructions to switch on the internal periscope heater and thus created the effect of a severe fog. Schultze felt that it must be possible to double the diameter of the head lenses to provide a better performance.

The speed indicator and navigation equipment were prone to too many breakdowns, making it exceedingly difficult to work out positions. In fact the naval system proved so useless that fishing charts, with accurate depths, and the echo sounder provided the best aids for finding the way home from the west of Ireland. He also said that it was essential to remember that the magnetic compass must be compared with the gyrocompass at least once every four hours. Especially large variations occurred after torpedoes had been discharged and the possible danger from this fluctuation must really be included in the training manuals, rather than be left for individuals to find out the hard way.

It was possible to use the 88mm deck gun as long as the sea was not too rough, but this was hardly advisable since it produced such insignificant results. Schultze said that it was necessary to take the speed of both the boat and the target into account, but the upper deck was usually so slippery and pitching and rolling, that it was extremely difficult, if not impossible, to calculate this accurately. For most of the time, he felt it was criminal to order the gun crew into action because injuries were too severe. Men were frequently swept off their feet to crash into harsh protrusions, making the transfer of heavy ammunition, loading and aiming too risky. Schultze also felt that the old anti-aircraft gun, fitted to the upper deck, aft of the conning tower, was virtually useless as well. Shortly after the beginning of the war, it was moved onto a platform to the rear of the conning tower, where he expected it to produce better results. During the first four months of war, this weapon was used only for stopping ships and occasionally preventing them from illuminating the U-boat with searchlights.

Upper deck torpedo storage containers proved quite useful. Moving the 1½-ton 'eels' down into the boat had not been too difficult, despite cold winter weather. However, the torpedoes themselves had given Schultze great cause for concern. There were too many failures, making him emphasise most strongly that not all of these could be put down to the firers having missed. There had to be some major fault with the mechanics. Many torpedoes simply did not explode but others detonated before reaching the target or shortly after having missed it, which obviously gave away the submarine's presence and put it at risk. Schultze pointed out that these faults must be rectified immediately.

He went on to say:

'The tactics of sending lone boats to operational areas at sea, which have been in use since the beginning of the war, are good as long as there remains such an abundance of independently sailing merchant ships. The fact that many of these are proceeding rather slowly has been an added advantage. Attacking convoys is somewhat different to what we had imagined before the beginning of the hostilities. The first detonation causes merchant ships to scatter in all directions over a wide area, making it exceedingly difficult to get into favourable shooting positions for subsequent attacks. This problem is made considerably worse by the presence of destroyers, which keep boats down long enough for the opposition to get a good head start. Consequently, it is quite difficult to catch targets for a second attack. Operating in shallow coastal waters is becoming noticeably more difficult as time goes on. Aircraft are the main nuisance here and the close proximity of land means that such support can be called up very quickly. Attempting to attack convoys with a group of submarines in shallow coastal waters appears to be pointless because the opposition reacts too fast. In view of these difficulties, it is necessary to create a weapon with which surface craft can be attacked while the submarine is deep in the water. I think some type of rising mine or a torpedo with a sound detecting sensor should meet the requirements. This really needs to be considered to be a necessity, which is required as soon as possible so that a "blind" submarine can shoot from depths of 20–25 metres.
'One's own realisation that a surfaced submarine is virtually impossible to spot in poor light comes rather slowly with experience. At night submarines are actually invisible and one must use this advantage to attack the opposition. Convoys and ships which may be attacked without warning are definitely the most vulnerable targets. Our night binoculars appear to be much superior to those used by the enemy. It often seems to be the case of us being able to see surface ships very clearly, while their inferior optics make it impossible for them to see us. Even after a

submarine is spotted head on, it offers such a tiny target that there are still ample opportunities for a successful attack before merchant ships take evasive action. It is important to use the large deck gun only when the opposition is unarmed or has clearly demonstrated that their shooting is considerably inferior to our own. At times, when the artillery officer gets it right and does not forget important parts of the routine, then the 88mm gun can have a significantly uplifting effect on the morale of all the crew. However, using the big gun will always expose the boat to additional danger and it is essential to keep eyes focused on the uninteresting parts of the horizon, while such an intensely enticing bombardment is going on.'

The trouble with torpedoes, mentioned briefly by Herbert Schultze, was to become a major issue for the first winter of the war. Initially, Dönitz dismissed negative reports by putting the abnormally large number of failures down to nerves. After all, none of his men had previously attacked in real anger while facing life-threatening situations, so he considered this to have been a significant part of the problem. However, it soon became clear that the fault lay not with the men, but with the machinery. This crisis was made considerably worse by the fact that German torpedoes were plagued by three different, but interrelating, faults and it seems highly likely that this appalling combination was not fully recognised until after the end of hostilities. This sad state of affairs was to cost the U-boat arm dearly and, in the spring of 1940, brought with it the fear of a possible rebellion. Such thoughts were nipped in the bud by considerable backstage activity to find a remedy.

Cold winter weather, with salt water in Kiel and Wilhelmshaven freezing solid, turned the men's attention to other matters and helped to slow thoughts of organising wolf packs in the Atlantic. Then, when conditions were showing the first signs of improvements, operations against merchant shipping were brought to a standstill by orders from the Supreme Naval Command. All resources had to be used to prepare for the invasion of Norway and Denmark. It is interesting to note that this was also the first time that Royal Air Force reconnaissance aircraft reached Kiel, where they took stunning three dimensional photographs of the busy harbour. But, having nothing to compare this with, Britain could not draw any conclusions from the evidence and it was not until the invasion was under way that London realised what was happening. U-boats were allocated such a secondary, supporting role in this mammoth undertaking that the majority patrolled cold, empty seas, where they did not meet any targets. Yet, some U-boats did see sufficient action to realise that the torpedo faults had not been remedied and further modifications were necessary. All this was clouded by the inability of experts to identify the exact reasons for the failures and therefore considerable experimentation was necessary to find the right combination for achieving better results. It was not a good time for U-boats or for forming wolf packs.

Above: The Bant barracks during the summer of 2001. They had hardly changed since the war, and walking around them one felt as if one was likely to bump into the ghosts of U-boat men. The compound had been used for a variety of purposes since the military vacated it but it now lies empty, with a definite air of dereliction.

Above: Kptlt Herbert Schultze, commander of *U48*, the most successful U-boat of World War 2, during an official function at Germania Works in Kiel. This was the only German shipyard with a massive glasshouse type of hangar over its construction slips. Herbert Schultze was on the verge of setting up the first wolf pack of the war, when he realised that he did not have the same charts or the same radio code as the other boats around him and could not communicate with them.

Above: The landward side of what was once the U-boat base in Wilhelmshaven. It was visited by a small group of British and American 'Friends of the U-Boot-Archiv' during a magnificent summer's day in the year 2001.

Above: U97, one of the first Type VIIC boats, under Kptlt Udo Heilmann, showing the silhouette so typical of the early boats. The large deck gun, forward of the conning tower, was of 88mm calibre for this type and 105mm for the larger, ocean-going Type IX. Two bollards can be seen raised near the bows, and behind them is the T-shaped receiver of the underwater sound detection system.

Above: German torpedoes could be adjusted to detonate magnetically when passing under the target or by contact when colliding with the side. When working properly, the first mentioned had the power to break a merchant ship in two, as can be seen in this picture. However, the complicated magnetic mechanism failed for much of the time and the less effective contact pistols had to be used instead.

Above: U31 has just broken through a surface layer of ice. Ice was quite a problem for submarines because all of them had a number of delicate tanks and vents around the outside of the hull, which could be damaged by brushing against hard, sharp surfaces.

Right:
Korvkpt Werner Hartmann as Commander of the 6th U-Flotilla (Flotilla *Hundius*) wearing the Knight's Cross of the Iron Cross around his neck, which he gained while serving as commander of *U37* at the same time. It was planned that he should be the first person to lead a wolf pack, but the majority of boats never reached their designated patrol line.

Chapter 3
U–boats Bite Without Wolf Packs
May–December 1940

The U-boat war was negotiating quite well the mass of restrictions imposed by Hitler at the highest level to avoid antagonism with Britain, in the hope of paving the way for meaningful peace negotiations. It was only when a series of these were refused, and there were no further prospects of coming to terms with the uncompromising government in London, that the leadership in Berlin realised a long and bitter conflict was inevitable.

Whilst Prize Ordinance regulations had been exceptionally irksome for U-boats, the majority of these restrictions were nowhere near as frustrating as their own malfunctioning torpedoes. These were still dominating the scene after the Norwegian campaign, when U-boats ventured out, once more, into the vastness of the Atlantic. The intensity of action during the spring of 1940 meant that maintenance work, due before the invasion of Norway, was postponed and damage inflicted during this period increased the length of the queues at the repair yards. Consequently, it was May 1940 before any significant number of boats started venturing out into the convoy routes to the west of Britain. This meant U-boats had gone for three months without intelligence about the disposition of merchant shipping and many new questions had to be answered. What changes had taken place? Which routes were the convoys using? What type of air cover might one expect? What reaction might U-boats meet from escorts? And so forth.

Once more, these concerns were quickly eclipsed by the persistent torpedo problem. Victor Oehrn (U37), who had left Wilhelmshaven on 15 May to take up position in the old favourite location off Finisterre, dominated the air waves with news of four more catastrophic failures. Dönitz cursed everything and everybody, while his staff wished he would tone down his aggressive onslaught on the higher admirals. His second-in-command, Korvkpt Eberhard Godt, could see his boss being shunted sideways into a post where he was less of a nuisance. Grand Admiral Erich Raeder, the Commander-in-Chief of the Navy, had already sent a terse memorandum saying that the Commander for U-boats should concentrate on fighting the war at sea and not concern himself with technical matters, so the final chop might not be long in coming. Although Godt and Dönitz were of highly contrasting characters, the combination worked extraordinarily well, with Godt's calmness adding good support to Dönitz's boisterous extrovert nature, and he fully understood what his boss meant when he said that they needed a few successes to boost the flagging morale.

Strangely enough, as if by magic, these were not long in coming. Despite the catastrophic start to the new offensive, things suddenly, and most unexpectedly, changed for the better. Four weeks later, on 9 June, U37 returned to Wilhelmshaven with a good number of success pennants fluttering from the extended periscope. Torpedo failures still dominated the conversation, but the bogeyman had partly been tamed with special handling and particular care. Oehrn discovered that attacking had become considerably easier due to the majority of restrictions having been lifted. Passenger ships were still not legitimate targets, but all

other traffic in the exclusion zone around the British Isles had become fair game, making it unnecessary to stop ships and inspect papers before sinking them.

The other significant change in the state of the war — the German invasion of the Low Countries and France — was already under way when U37 had left port, and Oehrn was chugging back around the north of Scotland when U30 (Kptlt Fritz-Julius Lemp) became the first U-boat to be refuelled in an occupied Biscay port. This took place in Lorient on 6 June 1940. Access to the French Atlantic ports reduced the trek between Germany and the convoy routes by a minimum of four days and, on top of that, made it unnecessary to negotiate the dangerous waters around the north of Scotland, where both the Royal Navy and Royal Air Force had changed from being a dire nuisance to a deadly threat. The availability of new bases was just the type of morale booster required by the U-boat Arm to make the prospects look so good that even the disastrous torpedo failures were pushed into second place. Many men felt the mechanical problems would soon be overcome, boosting them with a powerful urge to get to sea, to do their duty and to experience the mysterious romance of the French Atlantic coast.

At the same time, in the light of recent experiences, a number of officers were busy dissecting the *U-boat Commander's Handbook* and the old prewar rules. Much of this discussion centred around the remark by Herbert Schultze of U48 that a surfaced U-boat was so small that it was virtually invisible at night. He was not the only one to have noticed that submarines were so low in the water that the average British binoculars could not pick them out in poor light. This most positive advantage was not discovered as a result of daring bravado, but by accident, after a number of boats came unintentionally close to the opposition. Finding there was no retaliatory action, the men argued that, if this were possible, then why not exploit the situation by going in so close on the surface that they could guarantee a hit with a single torpedo. So far, the rules suggested it would be better to shoot a salvo of two, three or even four from a considerably longer distance of three kilometres. A 'sea-going' Type VII carried a maximum of 14, and an 'ocean-going' Type IX 22 torpedoes. So this proposal provided each boat with a considerable increase in hitting power.

The proposition of the short-range attack on the surface was especially attractive to men in the small Type II boats, who now saw themselves as being able to strike a significant blow in the North Atlantic. The basic design of these coastal 'dugouts' had been modified by stretching the hull and thus enlarging the fuel bunkers to provide a range of 6,000 nautical miles (over 11,000 kilometres), but without improving the torpedo capacity. These tiny boats were equipped with three bow tubes and carried only two spares, so their five torpedoes gave them a most limited hitting power. It was technically possible to stow a third in the central passageway, but the additional weight was such a nuisance during bad weather that this was not done very often. So far these boats had been employed in the thankless task of patrolling the North Sea with occasional sorties to lay mines close to British harbours. The first mentioned role did not bring many results, other than quick retaliation from aircraft, and the other was downright frightening. Now, the combination of the short-range attack at night and the availability of French bases offered them a new lease of life. To make matters even worse for Britain, these small boats were manned by well trained, enthusiastic young men, who were prepared to put up with every discomfort to reach their objective.

Early in June 1940, Kptlt Günther Prien (*U47*), the hero of Scapa Flow, was still on his way to the operations area off Cape Finisterre when German decoders in the B-Dienst (short for Funkbeobachtungsdienst — Radio Monitoring Service — under Heinz Bonatz) discovered convoy HX48, running eastwards from Halifax in Nova Scotia. Deciding that this was too good an opportunity to miss, Dönitz established a wolf pack to intercept it. However, the British did not oblige and their ships followed a more northerly route than expected to avoid the close proximity of the French bases. In any case, there wouldn't have been much to write home about, even if the censor would have allowed it. The majority of the U-boats never reached their allocated patrol areas.

At about the same time, the B-Dienst discovered another convoy containing at least three large liners, including the prestigious Cunarder *Queen Mary*, and escorted by the battlecruiser HMS *Hood*. Although this group was known to be proceeding at a minimum of 17 knots, roughly the same as the maximum for a U-boat, a pack was established in the hope that this rich prize might stumble in front of torpedo tubes, perhaps to repeat Otto Weddigen's hat-trick of World War 1, when he sunk three armoured cruisers in quick succession. Chasing such fast ships would have been futile, but there was always the slim chance that the British ships might stumble into the pack. On this occasion, no one was surprised that the Rösing pack did not meet its fast targets.

Hans Rudolf Rösing was commander of the 7th U-Flotilla in Kiel, when Kptlt Herbert Schultze of *U48* was admitted to hospital and no other 'hard nut' could be found to take Schultze's place. At the same time plans were being made to move the 7th Flotilla to France, so Rösing was travelling in the right geographical direction when he took *U48* out into the Atlantic and on to its new base, first in Lorient and then St Nazaire. Heinrich 'Ajax' Bleichrodt, who later replaced him, said the officers and men of *U48* were a wild bunch, who did not take kindly to inexperienced beginners. The average new commander was likely to face an exceedingly harsh ego collapse, ending up with serious doubts as to who was actually in charge. Looking at the log, it appears as if Rösing was happy to go along for the ride and to supervise attacks. The crew was so well trained that everything functioned perfectly well on its own and he didn't even sign the log book, leaving the general running to the first watch officer, Leutnant zur See (LtzS) Reinhard, but better known as 'Teddy', Suhren. Even Bleichrodt's exceptional character was, at times, left in doubt about who was actually in charge. On one occasion, while watching a fast ship disappear over the horizon, he declared that they did not stand a chance of getting it. Suhren cursed him dryly, saying they had caught faster things further away and asking for permission to shoot a single torpedo. Bleichrodt agreed only to prove Suhren wrong and was utterly amazed when he heard a detonation at the end of an exceptionally long run.

Below: One problem with using contact pistols in torpedoes was that this often blasted only a comparatively small hole in the side of the ship, meaning it took a long time to sink. There were numerous incidents where cargo, especially oil, spilled out through the hole, making the ship lighter and therefore causing it to lift the hole above the waterline. When ships toppled over slowly, as seen here, the merchant crew often had difficulty abandoning ship because the angle of the decks made it impossible to launch lifeboats.

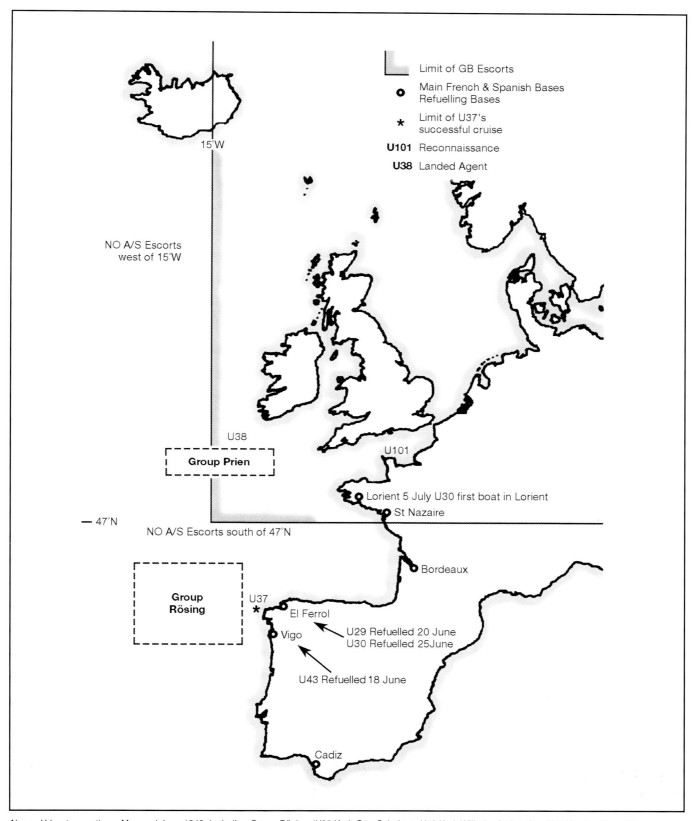

Above: U-boat operations: May and June 1940, including Group Rösing (*U29* Kptlt Otto Schuhart, *U43* Kptlt Wilhelm Ambrosius, *U48* Korvkpt Hans Rösing, *U46* Kptlt Engelbert Endrass and *U101* Kptlt Fritz Frauenheim) which attempted to intercept convoy US3, 12–15 June, and Group *Prien* (*U25* Kptlt Heinz Beduhn, *U28* Kptlt Günter Kuhnke, *U30* Kptlt Fritz-Julius Lemp, *U32* ObltzS Hans Jenisch, *U38* Kptlt Heinrich Liebe, *U47* Kptlt Günther Prien and *U51* Kptlt Dietrich Knorr) which attempted to intercept convoy HX48, 12–15 June.

Above: One of the small, coastal Type II boats with a 20mm gun forward of the conning tower. The lounging nature of the men would suggest that this was taken in a safe location somewhere within the confines of the Baltic, but a small number of these 'dugouts' made their way into the shipping lanes of Britain's Western Approaches. Type II boats were fitted with only three tubes and usually carried only two spare torpedoes, making such voyages hardly cost-effective and therefore it was not long before the majority were allocated to training flotillas.

Britain responded to the realisation that the new German bases in France were located on the very doorstep of action by rerouteing its convoys further north and effectively closing the majority of Channel ports. This gave both Liverpool and Glasgow a new importance and, at the same time, offered opportunities for the smaller harbours along the west coast. Although this lengthened the distance U-boats had to travel from France, it also helped them considerably because the traffic now had to funnel into a relatively narrow channel between Scotland and Ireland. This was indeed such a vulnerable constriction that Britain reduced its already overstretched naval and air commitments in other areas to provide cover for the still poorly protected convoys. Up to this period of time, U-boats had got used to meeting aggressive air patrols in the North Sea, especially in the Orkney–Faeroe passage, but it was going to be a while before these same teeth started biting in the Western Approaches. One reason for the slow start was that the vast majority of airmen had been firmly entrenched in land-based civilian careers, until shortly before being called upon to patrol the seas, and it was going to take a while before this willing reserve became accustomed to the hardships and confines of flying in precarious aircraft.

Despite the precautions taken to defend the convoy routes, Britain was surprised by an unexpectedly high number of attacks and by the inability of escorts to locate U-boats. At first, no one knew what was happening and a number of wild guesses had to be made, such as that they approached at periscope depth and made off at an incredibly fast underwater speed. Asdic, the device for detecting submerged submarines, could not locate boats close to the surface because of the turbulence of the water, and it took a while before it was realised that U-boats were travelling on the surface, where asdic did not work at all.

On 21 September 1940, when convoy HX72 was hit with the most severe loss of 11 merchant ships, the Royal Navy guessed that U-boats were not only approaching on the surface but also that they were faced with more than a single attacker. Following this, it was not long before the highly secret, monthly British Anti-Submarine Reports published a fairly accurate account of the U-boat tactics. These stated that U-boats were shadowing convoys by sailing on their beams until darkness provided the necessary cover to approach on the surface. Travelling at high speed, they selected their targets from point-blank range, fired their torpedoes and then made off, to vanish into the emptiness of the night. Boats with stern tubes fired another 'eel', as the German crews called them, while departing. Following this, if weather allowed, they reloaded on the surface, to be in a position to attack again before daylight brought an end to their monstrous activity. Initially the Royal Navy underestimated the number of U-boats, thinking that they were faced with two, perhaps three, when five had actually approached at more or less the same time.

This depressing news of the heavy losses was partly hidden from naval officers by emphasising successes rather than concentrating on losses. For example, the secret Anti-Submarine Reports mention, in some detail, how *U101's* (Kptlt Fritz Frauenheim) attack on HMS *Fiji* failed and how the 8,000-ton cruiser reached port despite having been hit. It was thought that the cruiser might have collided with the U-boat, since a loud clanging noise was heard, but it is more likely that this was one or two torpedoes hitting the target without detonating and thus adding to the statistics for those catastrophic failures. The Anti-Submarine Reports for the autumn of 1940 also gave new hope, saying the new invention of radar would soon make it possible to see in the dark. Some of this equipment had already been installed in convoy escorts, but teething problems were preventing it from functioning properly.

Despite an all-out effort to hit convoys, there were two major reasons for not forming wolf packs. First, there were hardly ever enough U-boats to make an effective patrol or reconnaissance line and, secondly, there were so many targets that U-boats would almost have had to make detours around merchant ships to reach their allocated areas. Merchant ships were so fast and furious in coming that many boats stumbled upon a convoy while heading towards merchant ships reported by another boat. This resulted in considerable confusion, especially during periods of poor visibility when the sun and stars were obscured for days on end to make navigation difficult. During this fateful period, there were hardly ever more than a dozen or so boats at sea and this number includes those on their way out and on the way home. So the total in contact with the opposition at any one time and with torpedoes still at hand was relatively small. Despite Britain being battered by, say, half a dozen or so U-boats, some historians have claimed that they almost won the Battle of the Atlantic, which is somewhat absurd when one looks at *Jane's Fighting Ships* and realises that the British Royal and Merchant navies were almost as big as those of the rest of the world's fleets put together. Surely it is foolish to suggest that half a dozen U-boats at sea could wipe this incredible power from the surface of the oceans?

The short-range surface attack at night started making its deadly impact once the first problem with torpedoes had been overcome. Torpedoes still gave rise to concern on 21 June 1940, when *U47* (Kptlt Günther Prien) fired three torpedoes in two minutes at convoy HX79 but succeeded in sinking only the 13,046 gross registered tons (grt) tanker *San Fernando*. Two other 7,000grt targets didn't even notice they had been in the sights of one of the most famous submarines of all times. Although simultaneous hits on two targets increased in frequency, it was not until shortly after midnight on 24 August 1940 that several targets being hit during a single attack were first seen, and this was especially remarkable since it was achieved by a small coastal boat of Type IIC with only three torpedo tubes. *U57* (Kptlt Erich Topp) fired, hit and sank three ships from convoy OB202 in a matter of a few minutes. (The ships sunk were the 5,681grt *Saint Dunstan*, 10,939grt *Cumberland* and 5,407grt *Havidar*.) The following night, *U124*, an ocean-going Type IXB under Georg-Wilhelm Schulz, almost matched this performance between 23.51 and 23.56 hours by firing three torpedoes in five minutes at convoy HX65A, but only two of the ships were sunk. (These were the 5,169grt *Harpalyce* and the 5,394grt *Firecrest*.) Four days later, *U100* (Kptlt Joachim Schepke) improved on this by sinking five ships from convoy OA204 between 00.23 and 04.27 hours. (*Hartismere* 5,498grt, *Dalblair* 4,608grt, *Astra II* 2,393grt, *Alida Gorthon* 2,373grt and *Empire Moose* 6,103grt.) The short-range surface attack at night had started to make a most significant impact. It became a raging success.

The point made earlier by Herbert Schultze, that of convoys scattering once attacked, no longer applied. Now, during the autumn of 1940, merchant ships maintained their steady columns, despite a succession of attacks. However, U-boat commanders reported that escorts started becoming highly frisky once they were alerted and the situation became quite tricky if this resulted in a fire illuminating the scene. This then became the hallmark of the so-called 'Happy Time'. There were times when two U-boats fired simultaneously at the same ship and even today, with log books from both sides, it is still difficult or even impossible to work out the exact sequence of the carnage.

U-boats benefited considerably from the Royal Navy being so short-handed that escort commanders were not allowed to hunt U-boats to destruction. Instead they were told to put submarines down and then take up their positions again around the outside of the convoy, with the hope of driving away other boats as they made their approach. But the long dark nights, combined with choppy seas, made this such an exceedingly difficult task that many U-boats merely slipped between the warships to attack with impunity from within the ranks of the convoy and then, if discovered, dropped below it to make their escape. It was indeed the U-boats' 'Happy Time'.

Below: U-boat operations: September to December 1940. Convoy SC2 (53 ships) was attacked in the first week of September 1940 containing U28 (Kptlt Günter Kühnke), U47 (Kptlt Günther Prien), U65 (Korvkpt Hans-Gerrit von Stockhausen), U99 (Kptlt Otto Kretschmer) and U101 (Kptlt Fritz Frauenheim).
Convoy HX72 was sighted by U47 on 20 September 1940 by a group containing U29 (Kptlt Otto Schuhart), U32 (ObltzS Hans Jenisch), U46 (Kptlt Engelbert Endrass), U47 (Kptlt Günther Prien), U48 (Kptlt Heinrich Bleichrodt), U65 (Kptlt Hans-Gerrit von Stockhausen), U99 (Kptlt Otto Kretschmer), U100 (Kptlt Joachim Schepke) and U138 (ObltzS Wolfgang Lüth).
Convoy SC7 was sighted by U48 (Kptlt Heinrich Bleichrodt) on 17 October 1940 and directed to it a group containing U38 (Kptlt Heinrich Liebe), U46 (Kptlt Englebert Endrass), U99 (Kptlt Otto Kretschmer), U100 (Kptlt Joachim Schepke), U101 (Kptlt Fritz Frauenheim) and U123 (Kptlt Karl-Heinz Moehle).
Convoy HX79 was sighted on 19 October 1941 by U47 (Kptlt Günther Prien). U28 (Kptlt Günter Kühnke) and U48 (Kptlt Heinrich Bleichrodt) attempted to intercept the convoy.
Convoy OB229 was chased on 19 October 1941 by U46 (Kptlt Englebert Endrass), U93 (Kptlt Claus Korth) and U124 (Kptlt Wilhelm Schulz).

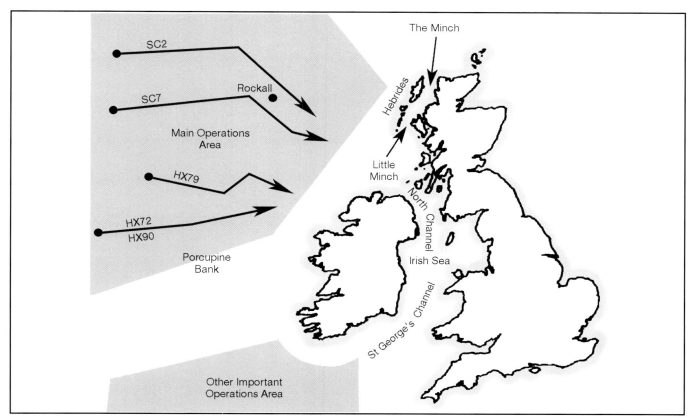

Right: This probably shows *U382*, a sea-going variety of Type VIIC, with an 88mm quick firing gun. The gun's delicate optical sight can be seen clipped onto the bracket above the hand-wheels on the left. Note that the large, man-sized bracket on this side has been turned outwards to support one of the gunners, so that he can use both hands to turn the wheel. The tampion at the front of the barrel had to be removed before the gun was fired. The emblem on both sides of the radio aerial intake shows Winston Churchill being squashed by two torpedoes and the snorting bull emblem of the 7th Flotilla can just be made out on the extreme right.

Below: *U181* with Korvkpt Wolfgang Lüth, one of only two U-boat commanders to be awarded the Knight's Cross with Oakleaves, Swords and Diamonds.

Opposite top: *U109* with Kptlt Heinrich — better known as 'Ajax' — Bleichrodt entering port. It was common for Bleichrodt to go to sea wearing his oldest clothes, but regulations stated that beards had to be shaved off once the men came into port, so he would hardly have left base with such a lush growth. Wolfgang Hirschfeld, *U109's* radio operator, identified the people in a similar photograph to this one in the U-Boot-Archiv and then finished with the poignant comment, 'but they are all dead'.

Inset: Finding trophies of war was difficult and the majority of boats had to satisfy themselves with boat-made flags flying from the extended periscope. This photograph was taken in November 1943 aboard *U415* under Kptlt Kurt Neide, indicating that an aircraft had been shot down.

Opposite far right: *U404* with Kptlt Otto von Bülow. Trying to identify the name on the lower success pennant is most difficult, since there does not seem to have been a ship with that combination of letters.

Right: Men relaxing on top of the conning tower of *U260*. Although hardly standing out against the white sky, there are three success pennants fluttering from the extended periscope. A machine-gun can be seen on the right and the special binoculars have been clipped on top of the torpedo sight. The man in the foreground, wearing a life jacket, is Torpedo-Mechanikersmaat Herbert Müller.

Above: Both the emblem showing a runic symbol and the two trophies displayed over the 105mm quick firing gun indicate that this is *U103*, a large ocean-going Type IXB. The 4,253grt SS *Wray Castle* from Liverpool was sunk on 3 May 1941 and SS *Elmdene* a month later, on 8 June, while *U103* was under the command of Korvkpt Viktor Schütze.

Above: Kptlt Fritz Frauenheim of *U101* shortly after having received the Knight's Cross. Frauenheim was one of the old lags, who joined the U-boat Arm long before the beginning of the war. He served as U-boat and Flotilla commander and became Chief of Staff with the Midget Weapons Unit towards the end of the war.

Chapter 4

The Start of the U–boats' Decline

November 1940–March 1941

The spring of 1941 saw some dramatic events. First, a number of 'Star Turn U-boat Commanders', as the Royal Navy called them, were lost during March and, secondly, the period saw a steady decline in the sinkings achieved by individual submarines. This deterioration has often been well hidden among the general war statistics by a rise in the number of merchant ships lost. Although sounding highly contradictory, these statements are both true. The reason for the difference is that the majority of historians have looked at the demise of merchant shipping without taking the number of U-boats at sea into account. Since the number of submarines increased dramatically until the summer of 1943, one would expect a corresponding rise in the number of merchant ships sunk and to appreciate the decline of the U-boats' effectiveness, one must convert the indigestibly large figures of tonnage sunk into the number of ships lost. Although these figures then become more manageable, they still include a slight distortion inasmuch that one is also counting a few tiny, insignificant boats, whose loss

hardly influenced the outcome of the war. When dividing the number of merchant ships sunk by the number of U-boats at sea, one is likely to get the best impression of the U-boats' performance. Those figures were used during the war by the U-boat Command to monitor progress and they are given in the appendix. They show, quite clearly, that from the autumn of 1940 onwards, there was a steady decline in the number of ships sunk per U-boat at sea.

The problem with battle statistics which many historians have used is that the U-boat Command had a totally different set of information at its disposal. Merchant ships losses, for example,

Below: Stores and provisions usually arrived by the lorry-full, to be dumped on the pier for the crew to sort out. The majority of the cases were too large to fit through hatches and, in any event, there was no room for excess baggage, so all unnecessary packing had to be removed. Stores were stowed carefully so that individual items could be found again. This meant everything had to be stowed in the reverse order in which it was going to be required and detailed location notes had to be made.

were generally estimated to have been at least one third higher than they really were. There were several reasons for this. Torpedo faults meant that some exploded harmlessly, some damaged ships did not in fact sink as the submarine commanders believed, and commanders were prone to overestimate the size of their targets. In addition to this, there is one further anomaly to bear in mind. Commanders at sea were loath to use the radio, not because there was a fear of being intercepted by British code-breakers, but because they were afraid of being detected by radio direction finders. Therefore, boats tended to remain silent until such time as their position had become known. So a series of individual sinkings, where the victims had not used their radio, was often not reported until a major attack was made on a convoy and then the boat was likely to report the total successes. The land-based U-boat Command sometimes assumed all these ships had been lost in a single convoy attack, thus giving a distorted view of the battle until after the commander came back to report in person. The interesting point is that earlier remarks and calculations in log books were usually not modified to take this new information into account.

Below: Conditions like these were not uncommon in the Atlantic, where waves frequently washed over the upper deck. In this case the boat is trimmed for quick diving though it would be possible to raise it slightly higher by blowing all of the tanks. Yet, this would be only a small help for the gun crew, who would still have had to cope with slippery decks. In any case, raising the boat higher in such stormy conditions would not have prevented the upper deck from being awash.

Readers who have grown used to looking upon May 1943 as the decisive turning point in the war must think again and realise that it is extremely easy to sink submarines. All you have to do is to drop a depth charge or bomb on them, and these devices were pretty old; they had already been available during World War 1. The tricky part of the process was to drop the weapon on exactly the right spot, and finding that small area where the submarine was lurking was the decisive problem during World War 2.

It is also worth considering that mankind usually needs a scapegoat when things go wrong and a hero when they go right. Consequently one person tends to get all the blame or praise while his backing team is often forgotten. Could the subconscious mentality behind this also be the reason why so many historians have looked in isolation at only one or two contributors to the Battle of the Atlantic? Headlines such as 'Radar has Won the War' and much later 'Enigma was Decisive' appeared to make the unwary think everything hinged on one factor. Yet, however good and important any one of these individual components may have been, it could never have had an effect without all the others. Therefore, to understand what happened at sea, it is necessary to look not only at a couple of great heroes but also at a vast number of tiny, and in themselves apparently insignificant, contributors. And a motley collection of these started to make themselves felt during the early spring of 1941.

The U-boat losses during March 1941 came as a great shock to the Germans. Sinkings had been running at the expected level of one or, occasionally, two boats per month, with none at all lost to enemy action in September 1940 and in January and February 1941. Then, in March, this total suddenly shot up to five, including three famous commanders. The loss of national heroes, such as Günther Prien, Joachim Schepke and Otto Kretschmer, was a shattering psychological blow, so serious that it took a while before the Supreme Command of the Armed Forces announced the news to the nation. And then it was wrapped up in a number of apparent successes. Today, one needs to look beyond the emotions to consider whether these losses were indeed a significant factor affecting the efficiency of the U-boat Arm. In fact it is likely that these successful men would have been withdrawn from front-line service, had they not been sunk. After all, all three had been at the centre of action since before the beginning of the war and a significant number of their contemporaries were shunted into non-combat jobs to work in offices within the U-boat Command, became land-based flotilla chiefs, joined training establishments or suffered mental breakdowns due to the 'unnecessary' and incessant pressure put upon them by their leaders. The word unnecessary is in inverted commas to emphasise that this is not the author's judgement, but the opinion of 'Ajax' Bleichrodt, one of the ace commanders, who suffered a mental breakdown at sea and was probably the only officer, throughout the entire war, to resign during mid-operation and to announce his intentions over the radio for all to hear. To understand the significance of this remark, it must be emphasised that Bleichrodt was definitely no also-ran but a holder of the Knight's Cross with Oakleaves, ranking among the top 15 commanders.

An interesting, and now often overlooked, point is that the 'tonnage king', Otto Kretschmer, the most successful U-boat commander of the war in terms of shipping sunk, was lost during the 19th month of war and the fighting continued for another 50 months or for over four years after he was sunk. Three months later, in June 1941, the most successful boat of the war (*U48*) fired its last torpedoes in anger, to be

withdrawn from active service due to its poor mechanical condition. This further helps to illustrate that U-boats never regained the initiative after the autumn of 1940 in terms of the fact that their individual successes declined steadily and rapidly from then onwards. This supports the view that the turning point in the war came early in 1941 and not in 1943, as so many have assumed. The argument that U-boats regained the offensive early in 1942 during the so-called 'Second Golden Time', when they attacked the United States, can be discounted. Those successes were achieved only because there were no convoy defences and no retaliation by the US until the summer of that year.

So what actually happened between the autumn of 1940 and the spring of 1941 to cause such a major change in fortune? The main calamity was that Germany had exposed every card in its hand, and it quickly became apparent that there were no more major surprises in stock. Never again were U-boats in a position to take the offensive and all they could do was to expose the weaknesses of their design and the inadequacy of the resources at their disposal. The flaws in the design were more significant than mere discomforts suffered by crews. They were to be decisive in the battles to come. The sad point is that much of this has hardly been recognised and therefore has not been taken into account when evaluating the war at sea. Once again, each individual failing may appear insignificant, but combine a number of them and one can quickly see that the composite deficiency made a significant impact on the U-boats' ability to fight a war.

The boats fighting the Battle of the Atlantic were basically World War 1 designs, built exceedingly quickly after 1935 to provide a glowing visual image of Hitler's rearmament programme. They lacked foresight and innovation, although this featured most dominantly in other German ship classes, especially in pocket battleships. Their underwater speed was so

Above: There were no hard and fast rules on how lookouts should be employed and each commander was free to devise his own system. Generally there were four men, each covering a quarter of the circle of vision, plus an officer or the Obersteuermann (navigator), who doubled up as Third Watch Officer. These men are wearing light rain gear, consisting of heavy coats and sou'westers. A magnetic compass can be seen in the foreground, attached to the periscope support.

slow that they were almost stationary when submerged, yet providing them with the power to attack convoys from below the waves was a simple matter of adding more batteries. This technology was already available in 1935, but then Germany failed to consider it for the new generation of submarines and therefore had to pay a heavy price for this neglect.

U-boats lacked effective reconnaissance facilities; they had no defence against small, fast warships and could not protect themselves well enough from modern, fast flying aircraft. On top of this, their main weapon, the torpedo, did not work properly. Professor Jürgen Rohwer has calculated that only about 10% of all acoustic torpedoes actually sank their target. The rest were failures. Dönitz's early claim that aircraft could not harm submarines was not only to be proved wrong but it also became quickly apparent that there was not enough space nor sufficient reserve buoyancy add more heavy guns to overcome this problem. Consequently aircraft became a major threat and there was very little U-boats could do about it. It must be remembered that the Kriegsmarine's U-boat fleet was originally built without any significant defence against aircraft and it was not until some years later that a few puny semi-automatic guns were added.

U-boats did not have effective ventilation, or heating or cooling systems. Whilst this did not play a major role until 1941, it was to prove the undoing of many when long dives became the order of the day and, later, when submarines ventured into exceptionally hot and cold regions. Ice formed

on the inside of some boats and there were other times when men had to endure temperatures like those of a moderately hot, but exceedingly damp, baking oven. Diesel engines provided a great deal of heat, but there was no way of transmitting this into the extremities of the boat. Diesels also sucked air into the boat, but that came down the conning tower and flowed on into the engine room, meaning that both the bow and the stern compartments remained unpleasantly stuffy. There were blowers, but these were not efficient and some officers found the air so foul that they hardly ever ventured into the cramped extremities where the ordinary seamen mainly lived and worked.

U-boats were without decent food storage facilities, making long cruises unbearably difficult. There was no place and often no fresh water for washing, nor any adequate lavatories. This last mentioned drawback could have been solved very easily by designing boats with waste water tanks, so that the men could use the 'head' whenever there was a need. Instead they often had to share one facility between 50 and even this could not be used all the time. High pressure systems, for when the boat dived deep, were not introduced until later and even then the

Left: Funkobergefreiter Günter Lorenz of *U43* sitting in a boatswain's chair attached to the sky or navigation periscope. Lifting a lookout higher in this ingenious way increased the distance he could see slightly, but such methods tended to be employed more as boat-made measures to overcome the frustration of not sighting anything, rather than as a serious attempt to see further.

Below: Keeping lookout during a raging storm was often impossible. The duty watch stood on the top of the conning tower, but their vision could be so restricted that they were travelling almost blind. Not only did deep waves prevent them from seeing too far, but the pain of spray hitting the eyes made this duty almost unbearable.

Opposite top: Probably *U393*, showing the torpedo sight in action. The special binocular sights were carried inside and were clipped in position only when required. The First Watch Officer usually aimed torpedoes while the commander kept an eye on the overall proceedings. However, this was not the 1WO's (pronounced 'One-W. O.') exclusive domain and some commanders as well as trainees on board shot as well. The man in the background is wearing some special goggle-like sunglasses with a flat front so that binoculars could be butted onto them.

Opposite bottom: The torpedo rooms at both ends were cramped and exceedingly stuffy. One commander remarked that he did not know how the men managed to live under such appalling conditions. Here, a torpedo has been winched up, ready to be pushed into the tube.

Left: U25, showing the torpedo room as living space rather than torpedo workshop, but even with all the 'eels' discharged, there was still very little room to stretch out.

Below: The torpedo room while the crew was sleeping. There were not enough bunks, but only the lucky ones managed to get a hammock. The rest had to make do with sleeping on metal floor plates with hardly enough space to turn round. Imagine having to get up to go to the 'head' (lavatory) under such cramped circumstances.

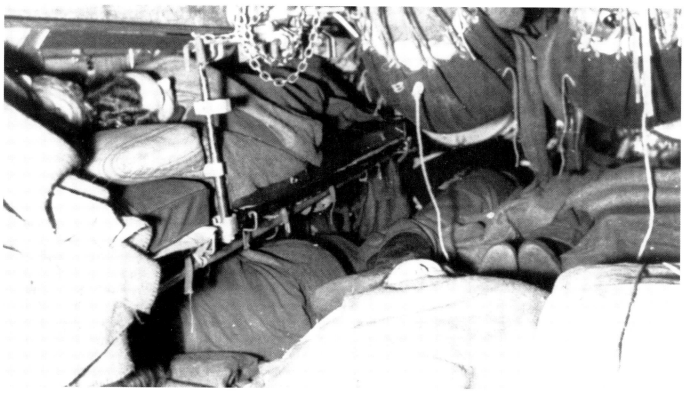

Above: These photographs from *U130* could show the 7,079grt Norwegian tanker *Malmanger*, which was sunk by Korvkpt Ernst Kals on 9 August 1942.

Above: Although sinkings became common, a good number of ships crossing the Atlantic did not issue all passengers with a life jacket nor saw fit to practise lifeboat drill until the critical moment when it was necessary to abandon ship. Others practised life boat drill under all conditions. Many survivors were in such pitiful states that U-boat commanders allowed only a minimum of the senior men on deck. The strange point about these frightful battles was that seamen from both sides found time for humanitarian aid, often helping survivors under exceptionally dangerous circumstances.

Top: Bearing in mind that the photographer had to be aboard a third vessel, it is quite likely that this is a friendly German ship close to a base, rather than a chance meeting on the high seas. However, it shows the type of merchant ship and submarine likely to be encountered during the Battle of the Atlantic.

Above and left: The end of a merchant ship, photographed from *U457* (Kptlt Karl Boddenberg).

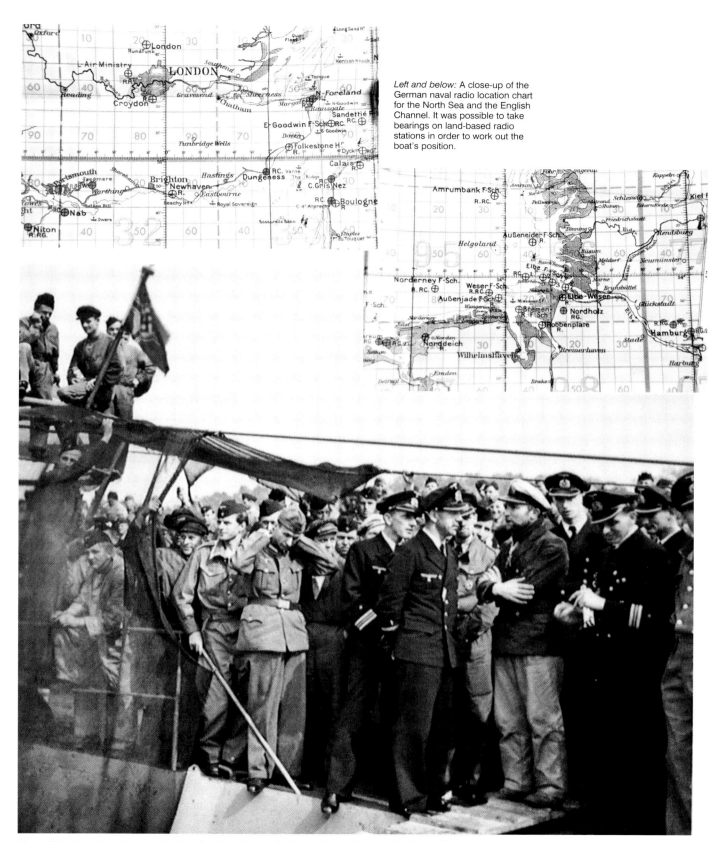

Left and below: A close-up of the German naval radio location chart for the North Sea and the English Channel. It was possible to take bearings on land-based radio stations in order to work out the boat's position.

Above: 'Star Turn U-boat Commanders', as the Royal Navy called them. On the right, in full uniform with the armbands of a Kapitänleutnant is the highest scoring U-boat commander of World War 2, the 'Tonnage King', Otto Kretschmer and to his left is the hero of Scapa Flow, Kptlt Günther Prien. The crowds present would suggest that this picture was taken after the beginning of the war, at a time when the two had become national celebrities.

Chapter 5

Disappointing Struggles

Books tend to give the impression that the war jerked along over a set of convenient stepping stones, with distinctive jumps between one and another, but in reality many events unfolded slowly through a swirling mist, while everything remained in constant motion. What is more, the key participants often did not notice the beginnings nor the ends of these phases. Even some apparently obvious markers created by historians, such as May 1943 supposedly being the turning point in the U-boat offensive, were not recognised at the time. Such cloudy vision was very much in evidence during the winter of 1940–1, when the decline of U-boat successes was initially put down to the seasonal bad weather. During February 1941, when a number of the old guard, including Kptlt Herbert Kuppisch (*U94*), came home from the once lucrative shipping lanes with a bag of three ships sunk for four weeks at sea, Dönitz concluded that the weather could not be the only cause. There was nothing else to point the finger at for the demise, but the number of boats drifting along the periphery of action was definitely increasing. This, in itself, was nothing new. Some commanders had always been unable to drive their attacks home by failing to get into shooting positions at the right time, even when conditions were most favourable, and it is worth adding that they were not 'also-ran dummies' but included a high proportion of sharp-witted individuals who later wore Knight's Crosses. British steps to protect vulnerable shipping were driving U-boats further west, away from the immediate coastal waters, but this had been predicted some time before and therefore did not come as a surprise. The mysterious element was that the emphasis of battle was slowly shifting away from attacking convoys to overcoming the difficulty of finding them. The few boats which did come close enough attacked with vigour to achieve startling results, but the proportion coming home without being able launch an attack increased so significantly as to make this a worrying factor.

We now know that the main underlying reason for this was Britain's introduction of radar, which made it possible to 'see' approaching U-boats, even during the darkest nights. But, when looking back at this period of time, it is important to remember that this invention brought with it a considerable entourage of problems. Men had to be trained, then they needed experience to make best use of their equipment, and initially there were numerous technical gremlins as well. All this resulted in the delicate apparatus failing at critical periods and inexperienced operators having difficulties distinguishing tiny U-boats among the clutter of echoes produced by turbulent waves. In addition to this, there were often not enough radar sets around a convoy to provide full cover. Instead there were gaps, through which U-boats could attack. So, although radar had made its first significant 'kills' by sinking the U-boat aces in March 1941, it was going to be a while before Germany recognised it as a deadly threat.

The difficulty of finding enemies at sea had always been a major problem and large warships were usually backed up by fast cruisers to act as eyes on the horizon. Even then, the coal-burning monsters of World War 1 had driven many men to despairing frustration rather than battle. Too often, empty bunkers had dictated a run back to port rather than an engagement with the enemy. The solution for this predicament could already be seen flying over coastal waters, but developing the eye in the sky was prohibited by the Treaty, or as it was known in Germany, the Dictate of Versailles, which prevented Germany from building or owning military aircraft after World War 1. In 1935 Hitler publicly repudiated the Dictate, saying he would no longer recognise its terms because the victorious Allies were not keeping to their side of the forced agreement. As a result, the previously prohibited weapons such as aircraft, submarines and large battleships were, once again, added to the German armoury.

Since Hitler's repudiation of the Versailles Dictate and his introduction of new defence laws also resulted in the founding of an air force, it seemed natural for this new institution to supervise the development of naval flying machines. After all, long-range flight over the oceans was still very difficult and the navy did not have trained airmen nor the industrial muscle to undertake such ambitious projects. This is not to say that the Naval High Command ignored its responsibilities entirely. In fact the opposite happened. A number of promising sailors, both commissioned and warrant officers, were seconded from sea-going duties to serve with the Luftwaffe in order to learn the tricks of the air. Some of these were killed during the early stages of the war and others remained with the air force, but a good number trickled back to the navy to give rise to some rather unusual clothing combinations. There are, for example, interesting photographs of men in naval uniforms wearing Luftwaffe awards.

Despite measures to create a naval air arm, the navy was hit a devastating blow shortly after the beginning of the war, when Admiral Raeder was told that technological difficulties with the naval bomber-cum-reconnaissance aircraft had resulted in the project being scrapped some years earlier, without the navy having been informed. As a small consolation, the navy's specifications for a multi-engine, long-range aircraft capable of flying over water with up to half its engines knocked out of action, were incorporated in a number of other designs. For example, an airmail service to South America was already in operation. Flying over such vast stretches of ocean was overcome by positioning floating refuelling stations in mid-Atlantic. Amphibious aircraft 'landed' on the water to be hauled up an incline onto the ship, refuelled and were then launched again by catapult. Such ambitious projects resulted in there being a number of long-range civilian aircraft, suitable for conversion into reconnaissance craft and able to fly far out into the British shipping lanes. However, relations with the head of the Luftwaffe, Reichsmarschall Hermann Göring, were not good, to put matters mildly. Consequently there was no smooth way the navy could lay its hands on the vital tools needed by U-boats to find elusive convoys. In the end, it was Hitler who intervened personally to bring a squadron of long-range Focke-Wulf Kondors under naval control. Today, it is well known that Göring was absent on a hunting trip when this happened and the consequent bickering and backbiting resulted in several unpleasant exchanges. Even after these had partly been settled, the results were not as good as the U-boat leadership had expected.

Above: People who are used to seeing container ports and roll-on roll-off ferries may have problems imagining what life was like during the war. In those days, docks all around the globe were still highly labour intensive, providing harbourmasters with real headaches when it came to dealing with convoys. A vast number of ships appearing all at the same time presented the system with many logistical problems, stretching both the labour force and the harbour facilities to the limit. The following photographs were taken in Hamburg, but they could just as well have been in any European port of the time and show how difficult life was for the ordinary dock worker.

Above: Goods were manhandled by an army of many thousands of labourers, often having to negotiate a labyrinth of hazards.

Above: Containers or large crates were still a rarity and a thing of the future. The majority of goods aboard ships came in all types of boxes and packages, all of which had to be manhandled towards the right destination.

Right: The crew usually did not participate in the loading or unloading of cargoes. Instead an army of dockers appeared, to work deep down in the holds. Threading these tyres onto a rope must have been a longwinded and labour intensive job, requiring energy and muscle.

Above: Work aboard ships, whether by crew or docker, was hard and not terribly well paid until after the war, when trade unions demanded such high wages that some firms went out of business. Although often classed as unskilled labour, a great deal was expected from the men who worked in, on or around ships.

Left: Britain overcame the labour problem aboard merchant ships by employing a high proportion of foreign workers for the mundane, unskilled jobs. Indians, like these parading on deck, were highly favoured because they were prepared to work long hours for little pay and they accepted quite appalling conditions without complaining.

Right: Managing and navigating merchant ships around the world was quite a complicated task and therefore high qualifications were demanded of the key personnel. Yet, much of the job involved working in excruciatingly difficult and often dirty situations. An inscription on the back of this picture states that it shows 3rd Mate Bailey and 2nd Mate Howdego of SS *York City*, but there appear to be no wartime records of the ship, so it probably went down or was withdrawn from service before 1939.

Below: Quayside space had already been a problem before the war, when many of the major European ports were struggling to cope with the masses of traffic seeking their facilities. Often there was no accommodation and ships had to be moored in midstream, where they were surrounded by floating cranes and lighters. This shows a mass of grain elevators emptying a ship in Hamburg harbour.

Above: Air traffic was still so much in its infancy that in effect it hardly existed. In those days only the very rich could afford to travel by air and, even then, there were very few long-distance routes. The majority of people travelled by ship, meaning it took several days to cross the Atlantic and weeks to get from London to the Far East. With most of the traffic floating on water, there was a wide variety of ship types. This shows the 10,086grt Blue Star Liner SS *Doric Star* from London in Port Said during March 1935

Above: The 5,487grt freighter *Wendover* shortly after it had been stopped by the German 'ghost cruiser' *Thor.*

Left: The 5,469grt freighter *City of Worcester*, belonging to the Ellerman Line of Liverpool.

Once at sea every ship became a legitimate target for the U-boats and it was a case of shooting before being shot at. This sequence was taken from *U130*.

Left: One of *U559's* victims burning fiercely, and therefore making it difficult for the crew to abandon ship. Yet, even in such dire situations, it was necessary to pump more shells or another torpedo into the wreck to prevent the crew from putting the fire out and limping on to port. There were even cases where sailors already in lifeboats reboarded their sinking ship with a view to trying to save it. Often, if there was time, U-boats waited for the crew to get clear before delivering the *coup de grâce*, but at night it was usually difficult to see what was going on and many men met a most horrible end.

Below: A ship burning at night.

Above: A model of a corvette on display at Bletchley Park, near Milton Keynes, showing one of the most common types of vessel used as convoy escort. Life aboard them must have been worse than in U-boats.

Above: The wartime 1,760-ton destroyer HMS *Norman* in the Pacific during April 1945. These 348ft (106m)-long ships were capable of 36 knots, making them more than a match for U-boats.

Chapter 7
Spies, Treason, Radio Codes and the *Bismarck* Disasters February–June 1941

Despite the navy having been the most security conscious of all the German armed forces, the U-boat Command carried out a thorough review of its procedures to establish whether the downturn of events in the Atlantic could be traced back to a leak in the system. This led to a further reduction in the number of men controlling the all-important convoy war and to the locking away of command maps showing positions of boats at sea. At the same time, the matter was discussed with representatives of the Supreme Naval Command, the aim being to reduce the flow of sensitive information to an absolute minimum. Yet, looking at this in retrospect one can see that the thoroughness did not penetrate terribly far. The Supreme Naval Command, for example, still sent U-boat positions in the Atlantic by 'safe' land-line to the Admiral commanding the Black Sea and to the Naval Command for the Balkans, neither of whom had the slightest interest in the information nor any need to know the locations.

U-boat positions were kept on a large operations map and since the autumn of 1940 they were also recorded each day in the U-boat Command's war diary. This most valuable document for historians was started on an *ad hoc* basis by the officers left in charge during the middle of August 1939 when the Three Front War Programme came into effect and Dönitz was still absent on leave. Following his quick return, the diary was kept running by recording a variety of events, but not in any special form. It was not until the beginning of November 1940, when Victor Oehrn (*U37*) was appointed to the position of 1st Staff Officer at the U-boat Command, that some standard pattern was established and the actual positions of boats at sea were recorded. This was no easy matter. U-boats did not report back to base every day, so the majority of these positions had to be estimated by a knowledgeable person who was aware of the individual orders and could guess what the commander at sea was likely to be doing.

Having ruled out the possibility of treason from within, the U-boat Command started looking around for opportunities where spies might penetrate. This was no easy matter. After all, the majority of operations started in occupied countries among an abundance of stories about espionage activities. There were prostitutes with beds permanently plugged into an open radio connection to London, even secret telephone links were supposed to have existed and then British submarines surfaced regularly off the French coast to receive the latest news from the Resistance via Morse lamp. Such stories ranged from the almost feasible to the totally ridiculous and, even if any of them were true, there was little the U-boat Command could do about it, other than hope that the Reich's official spy catchers might plug the odd hole. Dönitz was hardly intimidated by the scaremongering, hoping that his men had the sense not to disclose vital information. After a thorough investigation he was convinced that the leak was far more likely to lie in other quarters and it was not long before a likely source revealed itself.

This gremlin lay in the field of radio direction finding. This subject is deeply misunderstood today, especially since the emergence of secrets processed at Bletchley Park. A vast number of authors suddenly assumed U-boat commanders were afraid to use their radios in case their messages were deciphered in Britain, which is not true. Kptlt Otto Kretschmer was nicknamed 'Silent Otto' because he and many of his contemporaries were under the impression that Britain could determine the positions from which radio signals were transmitted. This fear became such a problem after the outbreak of war that Dönitz had to use his rather special form of cursing to get commanders to 'phone home'. Having established his land-based operations room, he found himself very much isolated by his old lags, who refused to tell him what was going on until their position became known through a victim's distress call. Time after time, Dönitz would tell commanders at sea that it was safe to use the radio once they were further than 200 nautical miles from land. Yet getting them to comply was like getting blood out of a stone. This fear remained with the men and immediately after the war KptzS Otto Köhler compiled a list of at least 50 U-boats which were sunk immediately after having broadcast a radio signal.

The necessity to keep information flowing if wolf pack operations were to succeed had just about got through to the most stubborn and most individualistic of commanders, when Dönitz had to postpone his lunch. The B-Dienst intercepted messages to suggest that U96 (Kptlt Heinrich Lehmann-Willenbrock) and U123 (Kptlt Karl-Heinz Moehle), acting as weather stations in the far western extremities of the Atlantic, had been detected by British radio direction finders. The error, if the news could be taken at face value, was considerable, and it produced an unsettling feeling that the British direction finders were better than presumed, and something had to be done to reinforce any possible weak link. Germany knew from gear found inside HM Submarine *Seal* (Lt-Cdr R. P. Lonsdale), which was captured in May 1940, and equipment left behind at the fall of France that Britain had made considerable progress with the field of radio location, and it was not difficult to guess that people had been working flat out to perfect the equipment.

The German backroom boys came up with the most helpful answer, saying they had no idea how Britain managed to find the positions! Being experts under the direct jurisdiction of the Supreme Naval Command, they suggested that there were so many anti-submarine forces at sea that sooner or later some of them were bound to run into U-boats. Such assistance left Dönitz none the wiser and, once again, forced him to introduce his own stopgap measures. These imposed further restrictions on the use of radio until such time as the position of the sender had become known to the enemy. At the same time he appointed a Radio Intelligence Officer to look for possible clues as to how Britain located U-boats at sea.

Sadly for the Germans, Dönitz had already driven a nail into his own coffin by being responsible for handing that most vital piece of information to the Royal Navy. This unfortunate chain of events started on 22 September 1940, when HM Submarine *Tuna* (Lt-Cdr Cavanagh-Mainwaring) sank the auxiliary cruiser *Atlantis's* prize *Tirranna*, while the ship was waiting for permission to enter the Gironde estuary. Two days later, *Tuna* also hit the Luftwaffe's ship *Ostmark*. This 1,281-ton tanker with catapult launching system for the air mail service to South America had been in position in mid-Atlantic at the outbreak of war, when it was ordered to take refuge in the neutral Canary Islands. It was in the process of being transferred from there to France when the Royal Navy struck right on the doorstep of the major U-boat bases. Dönitz was so disturbed by the thought that his U-boats were likely to be next that he introduced a system where outgoing boats sent a short signal when they reached 10° (later 15°) West to confirm they had reached the outer limits of the increasingly dangerous Bay of Biscay.

In Britain it was possible to determine the approximate latitude from which these signals had been sent and therefore Naval Intelligence could make a reasonable guess whether the boat was heading south, going into the Western Approaches or, later, making for the United States. Early in 1941 High Frequency Direction Finding (HF/DF) was still very much in its infancy but advances to the prototype FH1 meant that the more workable FH2 short wave D/F proved highly successful when fitted to warships later in the year and the invention was to make a major contribution to the war at sea. The reason it was so successful was that it could home in on Germany's short signals. These came from a special code book, which enabled quite long messages to be condensed into just a few letters of Morse code, much too short for conventional direction finders. U-boats usually reported the beginnings of their attacks and therefore a ship within a convoy could use HF/DF to determine the direction from which the approach was being made.

The problem with HF/DF, or Huff Duff as it was known, was that it took a while before sea-going personnel managed to cope with its intricacies. One Royal Navy commander even committed the unforgivable crime of reporting that his set was out action and asked for help to put it right. In doing so, he outlined exactly what the limited power in his set was achieving. This vital signal was intercepted and decoded by the German B-Dienst and handed to the U-boat Command. However, the radio expert (Korvkpt Hans Meckel) was kept so busy that he did not see the paper until after the end of the war. Earlier spy hunts had reduced the staff to an absolute minimum, so that only the smallest number of people were in the know about what was going on at sea. Consequently, everybody was driven beyond the limit and much of the routine paperwork just had to wait. Unlike in Britain, where Naval Intelligence grew in efficiency and importance, Germany's Central Naval Intelligence Division was founded in October 1937 and disbanded again during the middle of the war in favour of a decentralised approach. The higher authorities just could not see any value in a centralised authority for collecting information about their adversaries and much of this essential work was left to a few isolated officers in individual offices.

Continuous monitoring of procedures and actions at sea still pointed the finger at the possibility of the radio code being broken. Therefore, once again, Dönitz approached the experts at the Supreme Naval Command, who assured him there was no way anyone could ever gain an insight into the radio code, even if they had a captured machine at their disposal. The only possibility of the code being broken was if the opposition laid their hands on a machine set up for the day, but the settings were changed every day at midnight, so the ability to read the signals would cease pretty quickly. Much has been written in recent years about how Bletchley Park gained an insight into Enigma and it should not be necessary to go into details here, other than to mention that the machine was indeed a fantastic puzzle. Every book on earth could be coded with the machine, without having to use the same settings twice, so the German experts had good reasons for resting on their laurels. The important point to bear in mind is that the assurance of breaking the code being impossible made the situation considerably worse in that the volume of messages being transmitted to U-boats increased enormously and a great deal of unnecessary information was conveyed. For example, at one stage Dönitz reminded his commanders of the coming of a new moon and told them that the dark nights were excellent opportunities for attacking. Of course, the fear of direction finders continued, so the boats did not report back so frequently — signals from the U-boat Command were transmitted from known, fixed land stations, so the direction finder problem did not arise.

Despite the downturn of events during the winter of 1940/1, prospects for the future looked good. Hitler's decision shortly after the beginning of the war to increase U-boat production had already started paying dividends and there was a considerable increase in the numbers squeezing through the

Above: KptIt Claus Korth, Knight of the Iron Cross and commander of *U57* and *U93*, who found the survivors of the supply ship *Belchen* and brought them home against all odds.

training establishments in the Baltic. This had already shown up enough tight spots and shortcomings for the entire process to be streamlined by collecting together combat-experienced experts in specialised units to concentrate on specific aspects such as depth-keeping for engineer officers, artillery training, torpedo shooting and so forth. It was not only the training but also the kitting out of boats which was presenting enormous problems. After all, many of the new boats had inexperienced crews who could not decide for themselves what they should take to sea, and acquiring both hardware and food in sufficient quantities was not easy. To overcome this, a special fitting out facility, the 5th U-boat Flotilla, was established in Kiel under the leadership of Korvkpt Karl-Heinz Moehle (*U20* and *U123*) for the sole purpose of supplying everything a new boat was likely to need. Yet, despite this special effort, boats at sea still found tins stamped with a use-by date several months before they set out. Some tins were incorrectly labelled and others contained calamities such as cooked meats which had been burned before being sealed. Since virtually every U-boat after June 1941 passed through the 5th Flotilla, it must have been Germany's biggest. Moehle himself hardly features in history books, although he was a Knight of the Iron Cross. The probable reason for sweeping him under the carpet is that after the war the Allies sentenced him to five years in jail for passing on orders to commanders, something every military officer is expected to do. Such unjust action comes into the category of war events which have been actively suppressed and are now largely forgotten.

Both the increase in U-boat production and the streamlining of the training process meant that there were prospects of a dramatic increase in the number of boats appearing in the Atlantic. The average number at sea throughout 1940 was 13, and this included boats on their way out and on their way home, so the total in contact with the enemy was usually less than half a dozen. This figure remained steady until April 1941, when it increased to 19. In May it went up to 24 and for much of the remaining year it rose as high as 36.

To make the prospects even more challenging for the U-boat Command, this increase coincided with another significant event. The battleship *Bismarck* and the heavy cruiser *Prinz Eugen* were preparing for a joint commerce raiding operation into the North Atlantic. The big difficulty with this was that with both vessels, range had been sacrificed for speed and armament. Consequently both ships required a considerable consort of tankers to keep them at sea for any length of time. On this occasion the Fleet Command succeeded in dispatching 10 tankers, presenting the U-boat arm with a unique opportunity of striking in far-off regions. Unlike in earlier operations, submarines could now be distributed around the North and central Atlantic as far south as the Equator, allowing them to make surprise attacks in unexpected areas. The drastic reduction in the number of ships sunk during the preceding winter encouraged Dönitz to use this opportunity for exploring new operation areas.

It is worth adding at this stage that much of the western Atlantic was still out of bounds for the German Navy. Hitler did not want to antagonise the United States and therefore ordered the navy to observe the restrictions imposed by the so called Pan American Neutrality Zone. This included some Canadian areas because neutral shipping was running southwards to the States, but the northern areas, leading towards Britain were considered to have been fair game and the vast number of tankers provided the opportunity to hit at these out of the way locations.

The trouble with these plans was that *Bismarck* and *Prinz Eugen* left Norway on 21 May 1941, after having topped up their bunkers near Bergen, but less than two weeks earlier, on 9 May, a boarding party had entered *U110* (Kptlt Fritz-Julius Lemp) to capture an entire set of code books. The positions of the tankers were broadcast to U-boats at sea and consequently Britain not only took the glory for sinking the powerful *Bismarck* but soon also got nine of the 10 tankers, leaving a good number of U-boats in dire difficulties. This incredible success was later extended to the sinking of surface raiders and their special supply ships. Bletchley Park never succeeded in breaking into the raider code, because it was used so infrequently, but some of these ships carried supplies for U-boats and therefore their positions were also broadcast on the U-boat code. Consequently there were a number of sinkings, leaving both auxiliary cruisers and submarines stranded in the deep southern Atlantic. Although these units were in dire difficulties, a number of them managed to reach home. Others, such as the ghost cruiser *Atlantis* (KptzS Bernhard Rogge), were not so lucky. She was sunk on 22 November 1941, on her 622nd day at sea, without having put into a port. Contrary to many accounts, the ship did not go down with all guns blazing nor with the German war flag flying from the mainmast. The disguise was kept up all the time because Rogge saw no point in risking unnecessary lives against a much superior adversary such as the cruiser HMS *Devonshire* and thought it better for the Royal Navy to be under the impression that they might have sunk a harmless neutral merchant ship. The astonishing point about this incident was that the German Radio Monitoring Service intercepted the disguised distress call from *Atlantis* and was therefore instrumental in diverting the supply ship *Python* to pick up survivors. Britain also read these instructions and *Python* was sunk by the cruiser HMS *Dorsetshire*. At that stage a number of German and Italian U-boats came to the rescue, to bring the men back to France, where the majority arrived a few days before Christmas 1941.

Once again, looking at this in retrospect, this chain of events provides an easy to follow chapter in the history of World War 2, but at the time the whole period was shrouded in baffling confusion, with hardly anybody being in a position to provide a clear picture of what was going on. Yet, at the same time, U-boats brought home the evidence that their radio code had been compromised, but even this was not noticed among the bitter frustration of seeing well-laid plans disintegrate into featureless dust. From the German side it was a matter of reacting to one disaster after another or worrying about an acute silence in the ether. The High Command's doctrine that the position from which signals were transmitted could not be determined once the sender was further than a couple of hundred miles from land was not believed by a high proportion of commanders and Dönitz was well aware of this. Many of his top commanders cited incidents where U-boats were attacked shortly after having used their radios, so they preferred to remain silent and there was little he could do to induce them to switch their transmitters on. Even the frequent requests for their positions were often ignored.

This was very much the case when *U93* under Kptlt Claus Korth approached an isolated spot off the southern tip of Greenland to refuel from the tanker *Belchen*. Finding instead almost 50 survivors from the *Belchen* in lifeboats, Korth guessed that the position was still dangerous and therefore he saw no reason to broadcast the news and risk his own boat. The plus point was that *U93* had just about enough fuel to get back to France. As the number of survivors being picked up grew, it became obvious there was no opportunity of rejoining the *West* wolf pack and the situation with so many squeezed into the boat was so precarious that it would not withstand a depth charge attack due to the extra weight and difficulty of moving about inside. This put any prospects of further action out of the question and left Korth with no alternative other than to crawl back. The interesting point about this decision is that he did not inform the U-boat Command and on his way back came across a number of convoys. On each occasion a concerted effort was made to avoid contact because the large number of men on board would have driven *U93* to a certain death.

Once back in France, Korth was severely reprimanded by Dönitz for failing to report the convoys. He was told that U-boat wolf packs, stretched out across the shipping lanes, did not find any targets, yet he was sitting under several convoys and should, at least, have reported their presence. Reading this here could easily give the impression that Korth had a slight tiff with his chief because he also received the Knight's Cross at the same time. Yet, the effects of this incident must have been quite severe because it still troubled Korth 40 years after it had happened. In the late 1970s he went through the records in the U-Boot Archiv to reconstruct the events of that fateful episode, to establish whether he had taken the right decision or not. The sad point about this is that such a course of events was not unique. Several others broke off action due to heavy damage and then, while crawling back home, found they ran into an abundance of targets, but no one in the High Command noticed the pattern that every time boats were forced to make their own decisions they started running into convoys. It was only those boats whose positions were being broadcast which failed to find the enemy.

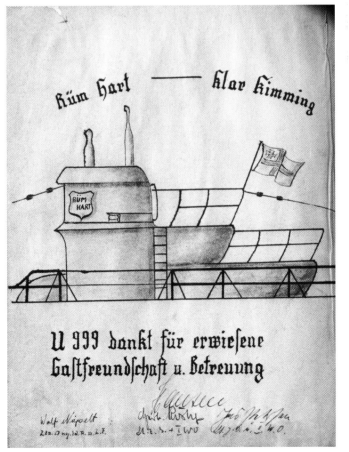

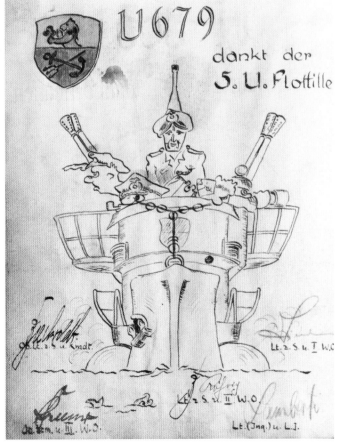

The second attack is even more mystifying. *U203* came in shortly before 03.00 hours, not long after the earlier commotion had subsided. Mützelburg fired two torpedoes at different targets and managed to remain long enough on the surface to observe the immediate sinking of the 2,475grt freighter *Hawkinge*. A second freighter, seen to have stopped while the crew abandoned ship, was reported as having sunk 20 minutes later, but there is no record of such an event from the British side. Could it have been a rescue ship, stopping to pick up survivors? Following this, the convoy was left in peace to nurse its wounds until shortly before 24.00 hours of the same day when *U126* attacked. Once again, all four bow tubes were shot virtually simultaneously at different targets. The boat turned and the two stern torpedoes followed a couple of minutes later. One ship exploded most dramatically while the First Watch Officer was still aiming. Seconds later, there was another detonation. Although the lookouts had now lost sight of their first targets, they did observe both the stern shots hit, but it looked as if only the last target started sinking. Remaining around for further verification of success would have been folly and Bauer made off quickly before escorts could prevent his escape. Lookouts recorded a total of four positive hits, but records show that only two ships were sunk. The fact that lookouts lost sight of the target ships can be explained by U-boats turning and twisting. Each of the four lookouts would have had a sector of about ninety degrees, so it was quite common for the one who saw a torpedo hit to be looking in a different direction a few minutes later.

Karl-Friedrich Merten was not so lucky. Approaching the convoy, he found *U68* confronted by a corvette, moving at the same speed as the merchant ships and obviously oblivious to the presence of the U-boat. There was a gap to get in, but that would almost certainly be snapped shut by the first detonation. Therefore Merten decided to sink the warship with his first shot, before turning his attention on the freighters. This resulted in an impressive sheet of flame illuminating the night air and in things becoming literally too hot for any further action. Therefore Merten abandoned his attack, hoping he would get another chance later on, but this was not to be.

The subsequent attacks by *U561* and *U203* are just as mystifying as the earlier efforts. Bartels reported a tanker bursting into flame and vanishing below the waves within 30 seconds. Yet, once again, Jürgen Rohwer has been unable to identify this apparently obvious target in his valuable book *Axis Submarine Successes of World War Two*. This would suggest that either the ship did not exist or has not been included among Admiralty records. Today, it is all too easy to put such reports down to the exaggeration of the commander and lookouts, but reports like these abound in great numbers, especially in the Mediterranean. It seems unlikely that men of such calibre would make up dramatic stories of ships sinking among a sea of flames if they hadn't seen them, and it would suggest that even today we are still faced with large gaps in the history of the war at sea.

Whilst this action against convoy OG69 may have been the first example of an aircraft successfully bringing U-boats to battle, the overall results were hardly sufficient to make an impact upon the all-important convoy war. The main problem was that there were too few aircraft to make any significant contribution. Far too often, it was possible to keep only a maximum of two on patrol and there were many days when that small number were laid up. Even with one flying a few hours after the other, it was impossible to keep convoys under constant surveillance, making it far too easy for the merchant ships to maintain their heading until darkness gave them the

necessary cover for a drastic change in course. The only advantage was that an ever-increasing number of boats were appearing in service, making it possible to establish two independent wolf packs in different areas, one between the west of Ireland and the south, and the other between the north of Ireland and the west. The reason for not concentrating all the boats in one area was that there had been a noticeable increase in British aircraft and Dönitz was intent on dividing this interfering force to lessen its impact.

The operational areas for August were chosen from an analysis of bearings taking by the B-Dienst over a period of time, suggesting the best areas where the merchant traffic was likely to be concentrated, but this proved to be quite disastrous on this occasion. The northern pack was made up of boats from Germany on their first operational cruise and even those from France, who had been on at least one previous voyage, did not meet with any noteworthy success. A few came within shooting range, but the overall results were very much similar to what had happened with convoy OG69. The nature of the failures convinced Dönitz that it was not an abundance of enemy forces, but something far more sinister, such as radar, which was defeating the attacks. Far too many U-boats got close to merchant ships, to be put down at the last moment by aircraft or the zealous escorts.

The fact that these aggressors were reported to be bearing down on U-boats at great speed when they were first sighted suggested that they had detected the U-boat long before lookouts on the conning tower had seen the escort. Up to this time, the situation had usually been the other way round. With the submarine's small silhouette being hardly visible, it was usually the U-boat lookouts who first saw the surface warships. The other most significant point was that these escorts were now appearing before the first U-boat had sighted the merchant ships and therefore making the shadowing process virtually impossible. During the summer of 1941, it became evident that it was no longer possible for U-boats to sail ahead or by the side of a convoy without being molested and therefore the only way for the pack to converge was for everybody to work out the likely position of the target from the first sighting report. This gave direction, speed and usually the size of the convoy, as well as the number of escorts. However, when clouds and gales made navigation difficult, it could well have been that none of the boats knew their exact position because they had been unable to take bearings on the stars or sun. Therefore navigation became an academic exercise of calculated guesswork which was not accurate enough for finding a relatively small target in vast mountainous seas. The absence of homing signals from the shadowing boat certainly added considerable problems, making it difficult for the pack to converge on the same spot.

At this period of time, in August 1941, the whole issue of how U-boats were detected was clouded by a massive anomaly. German radar research had been cancelled shortly after the outbreak of the war, when Hitler decreed that military research which could not be completed in the near future should be curtailed. Even while radar development was still in progress, Germany had slightly different views to Britain on the subject, as we have seen. Germany's decision to develop radar as a means of supplementing optical range finders during poor visibility, to be used after the target had been visually sighted, meant that radar sets were developed for installation aboard large ships for the purpose of finding other big ships. This gave German radio experts the impression that radar would not work from small vessels, such as convoy escorts, because the radar echoes from the surface of the sea would cause too much

Above: KptLt Reinhard Suhren of *U564* on the left.

interference. Support for this theory was provided when a number of U-boats reported the presence of a cruiser or large merchant ship within the ranks of a convoy, presumably being present as a radar platform to help the escorts. It is quite likely, however, that these were cases of mistaken identify. After all, it was not too uncommon for inexperienced lookouts to class a larger destroyer as a cruiser, especially when it was spotted in bad visibility close to a smaller escort.

In addition to this, the issue of how Britain found U-boats was clouded by a whole squadron of other possible solutions. For example, *U123* (Reinhard Hardegen) reported seeing a Kondor reconnaissance bomber a long way off, circling over what probably was another U-boat. His suggestion was that such action could advertise the presence of a whole U-boat pack over a vast area of ocean.

Obviously, the problem of not being able to find convoys demanded a new approach, but there was very little U-boats could do. Dönitz's immediate response was to point out that more U-boats were needed in the shipping lanes, but that would take a while to achieve and it was going to be another year or so before such numbers were available. So far, commanders had instructions to avoid attacking escorts, even if these presented a slow, 'sideways-on' target, the reason being that the escorts had been so ineffective that it was thought better to sink valuable merchant ships. However, this changed during August 1941, when Dönitz placed all small warships on the target list, telling commanders it would be necessary to eliminate the defence ring before gaining access to the more vulnerable merchantmen. This was no easy proposition because the U-boats did not have an effective weapon for the task. A fast, approaching warship presented such a small target that it was virtually impossible to hit with an ordinary torpedo. Therefore the U-boats' only chance was to get in on the act before being noticed, while still being faced with a 'sideways-on' target. Whilst this was quite hazardous, Dönitz took the risk because the increase in the

number of attacks against approaching U-boats had not resulted in a corresponding rise in the numbers sunk. Therefore it was thought to be a risk worth taking.

Of course, all these new techniques were nothing more than stopgap measures until new weapons would be available. These were: special anti-convoy torpedoes, called 'Curly' in Britain because they ran in loops once they had reached the merchant ships; an acoustic homing torpedo for tackling small, fast warships; and better anti-aircraft protection, radar detectors and radar foxers.

Looking at this problem from the British point of view provides an interesting insight into the dramatic change in the course of the battle. First, the reason why Germany had noticed an increase in the number of anti-submarine forces was that Britain was now reading the U-boats' radio code which meant Britain could employ its limited forces in exactly the right area for maximum effect.

In addition to this, some of the wolf pack attacks were already being frustrated by the new Huff Duff equipment, which had its first sea trials in July 1941. The significance of this most valuable invention has been somewhat undervalued, although it made an enormous contribution to the fight against U-boats. It was revolutionary because it could determine the direction from which even the short signals were coming. There was no need to rotate aerials or even to identify the signal. Matters were more complicated if an accurate position was required because then data from more than one station was necessary, but all this was not needed by escorts around a convoy. U-boats were ordered to report back to base the moment they were starting their attack, not so much to keep Dönitz informed about what was going on, but to prevent any possible calamities of one boat running into another. This meant that a convoy needed only one Huff Duff set to know that an attack was likely to begin shortly and the terrific bonus was that this also indicated the direction the intruder was coming from. Now, add radar and asdic and it is easy to see how these make a deadly combination.

Chapter 9
The First Fast Moving Patrol Line
September–December 1941

Above: HMS *Chaser*, a typical example of an escort carrier, was brought into service during the summer of 1942, after having been converted from the freighter *Mormacgulf*. Whilst such ships may have looked impressive, the early versions did not have hangars, meaning that their aircraft had to be stored and maintained on an open flight deck in all weathers.

It must be emphasised, once again, that the terrific successes achieved by U-boats during the autumn of 1940 were mainly due to close-range, individual surface attacks at night, rather than the employment of wolf packs. At that time it was possible for one boat to call in others for highly successful but unorganised group attacks. Historians seeking emotional drama rather than reality later labelled these with the sensational term of 'wolf pack'. However, it is most important to bear in mind that the first organised groups did not make a significant appearance until the spring of 1941 and it is necessary to distinguish between the earlier uncoordinated group attacks and the later wolf pack concept. The U-boat Command tended to use the term 'patrol line', 'reconnaissance line', 'group' or 'pack' for these organised groups, while the propaganda system referred to individual U-boats and men as 'wolves', whence it is not too difficult to be diverted to the dramatic name of 'wolf pack'.

During the autumn of 1940 various U-boats would converge on the same convoy after it had been sighted by one of them, but up to that moment in time, the group had usually not existed as a recognisable unit. Calling boats together was possible because most of the action took place over a relatively small area, fairly close to the British coast, where traffic funnelled into a comparatively narrow channel leading to the western ports.

Finding convoys during this period was not a major problem, since the abundance of shipping provided a multitude of targets.

This pattern changed dramatically during the first months of 1941, when the finding of convoys became a notable challenge, and the land-based Operations Room, which became known as the U-boat Command, co-ordinated the first proper patrol lines. Considerable debate had already gone into the exact composition of such groups, to create a system whereby the smallest number of boats could cover the greatest possible area. The chosen basic pattern was to form a line abreast across the path of an anticipated convoy. In theory, once in the line, each boat would cruise on a roughly parallel course to the expected merchant ships. The exact location of the patrol area was determined by aircraft sighting reports, by signals intercepted by the B-Dienst or rarely by a U-boat, and the distance between each boat was determined by the land-based U-boat Command according to prevailing conditions. Theoretically, these gaps were twice as wide as the visibility distance from a conning tower. This should have made it impossible for ships to slip in between without being seen. The disadvantage was, of course, that U-boats couldn't see each other and therefore had no visual check, and radio silence was maintained to prevent direction finders from locating the pack. The film *Das Boot* contains some rather poignant scenes where two boats meet during an appalling storm, indicating that there must be a vast gap elsewhere. A discussion between the commander and navigator then shows the difficulty of obtaining correct positions during periods of bad visibility, when it was impossible to take sights on the sun or stars for days on end.

By the spring of 1941 the U-boat Command's involvement had become a critical factor in the war at sea. Although the new commanders were still officers who had gone through the thorough prewar naval training schedules, a good number had since been hurriedly pushed through submarine and commander schools. This made it necessary to provide that essential guide, the *U-boat Commander's Handbook*, and for the land-based operations room to send a constant stream of elementary advice. Their inefficiency can be gauged by looking at the number of boats, at least 16, lost during their first operational cruise during the war up to this spring 1941 period. The surprising factor to emerge from this statistic is that 10 of them had also sunk at least one ship, suggesting they were lost while attacking.

Although the virtually static or slow moving patrol line, used throughout the spring and summer of 1941, brought nothing but disappointing failure, there was very little the U-boat Command could do to improve matters because there were too few boats to implement the obvious alternative. That was to assemble a patrol line and to keep it constantly on the move, making it much more difficult for enemy tracking stations. This proposition was formulated as early as April 1941, but not implemented until September, when the number of U-boats at sea had increased sufficiently. The major problem with this tactic was that it required a high degree of radio co-ordination from the land and, on top of that, each boat was going to consume considerably more fuel. Three months earlier Germany had lost nine out of 10 supply ships around the time when the battleship *Bismarck* was sunk and no one in Germany was keen on proposing that more should be sent into the North Atlantic. Submarine tankers were already under construction, but the first one, *U459*, was not launched until 13 September 1941, putting any prospects for prolonging cruises out of the question until the early summer of the following year.

By September 1941 it was obvious that the spring offensive, involving a return to the eastern reaches of the Atlantic, had been a mistake and this left the U-boat Command with no feasible alternative other than to head further west, towards the Canadian coast, or to evacuate the North Atlantic altogether. Moving further west brought with it the obvious additional disadvantage of using even more fuel and thus drastically cutting the time each boat could spend hunting convoys, but that was the price Germany was going to have to pay. Once again, the new effort further west was dominated by a lack of targets. This time aircraft managed to find an adequate supply of convoys, but each time the U-boats were too far away to reach them. Dönitz's son-in-law, Günter Hessler, remarked that

Below: Many of the escort carriers' flight decks were made from wood, making them somewhat slippery during wet weather. This is HMS *Chaser*.

it was very much a case of the U-boat Command reacting and adapting to the ever-changing conditions at sea, making it a real problem to evaluate what was actually happening.

The first fast moving patrol line assembled towards the south of Iceland with a view to sweeping westwards in a huge arc towards Cape Farewell, the southern tip of Greenland, at about 10 knots. This line was still being set up when the problem of identification arose. After all, soon there would be several packs at sea at the same time. So, to overcome this, the group was given the name of *Markgraf* (literally Border Count, best translated as Marcher Lord). Although sounding fairly innocuous in English, the German term was steeped in history and associated with numerous bloody battles. These counts lived in the border regions of medieval Germany, where they had come under constant attack from neighbouring countries. On this occasion, in September 1941, the name heralded an impressive success when the patrol line intercepted convoy SC42, even though the large gaps between the boats and the vast length of the north–south line made it impossible for all to converge for action. Despite the limited

contact, 20 ships were reported as having been sunk. In 1946, this figure was modified to 16 and Jürgen Rohwer lists 22 in *Axis Submarine Successes*, from an original convoy total of about 70. This was stunningly high, although the overall performance of ships sunk per boat at sea remained disappointingly low from a German viewpoint.

Once again, a variety of conflicting original reports make it difficult to reconstruct the exact proceedings, but a blow for blow account is hardly necessary for this book and it is far more interesting to note that every attacking boat reported an abundance of powerful escorts. Forming two rings around the merchant ships, they made it exceptionally difficult to approach close enough for launching torpedoes. In addition to this, an unusually large number of aircraft were recorded in an area which had previously been free from aerial interference.

This worrying presence of small aircraft was more than a mere nuisance and prefigured an important move to combat U-boats. Britain was now introducing two significant new weapons in this field. The more important was the escort aircraft carrier, at this stage made by merely adding a flight deck

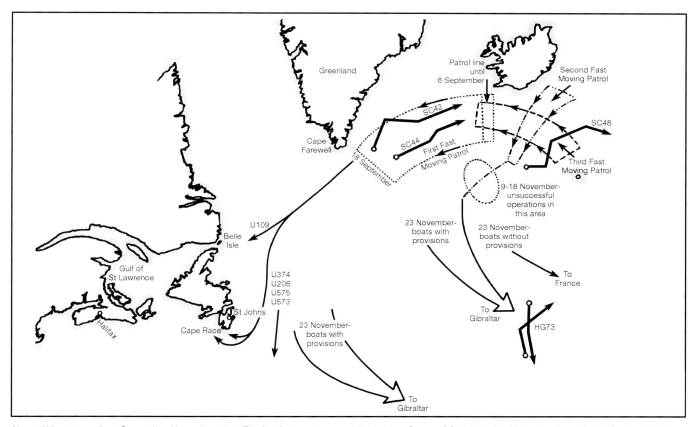

Above: U-boat operations September–November 1941. The first fast-moving patrol line against Convoy SC42 comprised *U38* (Korvkpt Heinrich Schuch), *U43* (Kptlt Wolfgang Lüth), *U81* (Kptlt Friedrich Guggenberger), *U82* (Kptlt Siegfried Rollmann), *U84* (Kptlt Horst Uphoff), *U85* (ObltzS Eberhard Greger), *U105* (Kptlt Georg Schewe), *U202* (Kptlt Hans-Heinz Linder), *U207* (ObltzS Fritz Meyer), *U372* (Kptlt Hans-Joachim Neumann) joined later, *U373* (Kptlt Paul-Karl Loeser), *U432* (Kptlt Heinz-Otto Schultze), *U433* (ObltzS Hans Ey), *U501* (Korvkpt Hugo Förster), *U552* (Kptlt Erich Topp), *U569* (Kptlt Hans-Peter Hinsch), *U572* (Kptlt Heinz Hirsacker), *U575* (Kptlt Günther Heydemann) and *U652* (ObltzS Georg-Werner Fraatz).
The return leg of the first fast-moving patrol line against Convoy SC44 comprised *U74* (Kptlt Eitel-Friedrich Kentrat), *U94* (ObltzS Otto Ites), *U373* (Kptlt Paul-Karl Loeser), *U552* (Kptlt Erich Topp) and *U562* (Kptlt Horst Hamm).
The following boats followed behind the first fast-moving patrol line and continued to reconnoitre Canadian waters: *U109* (Kptlt Heinrich Bleichrodt), *U208* (ObltzS Alfred Schlieper), *U374* (ObltzS Unno von Fischel), *U573* (Kptlt Heinrich Heinsohn) and *U575* (Kptlt Günther Heydemann).
The second fast-moving patrol line was established after the following boats attacked Convoy SC48: *U73* (Kptlt Helmut Rosenbaum), *U77* (Kptlt Heinrich Schonder), *U101* (Kptlt Fritz Frauenheim), *U432* (Kptlt Heinz-Otto Schultze), *U502* (Kptlt Jürgen von Rosenstiel), *U553* (Korvkpt Hugo Förster), *U558* (Kptlt Günther Krech), *U568* (Kptlt Joachim Preuss) and *U751* (Kptlt Gerhard Bigalk).
The third fast-moving patrol line against Convoy SC52 comprised *U38* (Korvkpt Heinrich Schuch), *U82* (Kptlt Siegfried Rollmann), *U84* (Kptlt Horst Uphoff), *U85* (ObltzS Eberhard Greger), *U93* (ObltzS Horst Elfe), *U106* (Kptlt Hermann Rasch), *U123* (Kptlt Reinhard Hardegen), *U133* (Kptlt Hermann Hesse), *U202* (Kptlt Hans-Heinz Linder), *U203* (Kptlt Rolf Mützelburg), *U569* (Kptlt Hans-Peter Hinsch), *U571* (Kptlt Helmut Möhlmann) and *U577* (Kptlt Herbert Schauenburg).

to a merchant ship but later purpose built. Ironically, the first of these ships, HMS *Audacity*, was the captured ex-German freighter, the *Hannover*. However, it would still be a while before these were regularly plying their incredible trade through the gales of the North Atlantic. Working on them, with aircraft parked and maintained on a constantly pitching and rolling open flight deck, must have been sheer purgatory. There were neither hangars nor a great deal of protection for the maintenance teams. It is a wonder that there were men brave enough to combat the natural elements to provide the essential protection for convoys. The second new weapon was designed as a stopgap while these escort carriers were being converted. This was to install an aircraft catapult on the bows of some merchant ships. The idea was to launch a pilot in an older, almost worn out fighter to tackle the German reconnaissance bombers, as well as any U-boats in the area. The pilot was expected to fly until he ran out of fuel and then parachute into the sea and hope that one of the ships he had been protecting would stop and pick him up. Today it is virtually impossible to imagine the courage these men must have taken with them into those hostile waters. The fact that many operations took place during the bad weather of winter months makes this performance even more remarkable.

Just to place these events in the sequence of time, the first CAM or Catapult Aircraft Merchantman, the *Empire Rainbow*, launched its first fighter during May 1941 and HMS *Audacity* began trials in June 1941 and escorted its first convoy in September 1941. The first Focke-Wulf reconnaissance bomber was shot down during August by an aircraft launched from the CAM ship *Springbank* of convoy HG73. This ship, in turn, was sunk by *U201* (Kptlt Adalbert Schnee) on 27 September. The first CAM ship to be sunk was the 7,465grt freighter *Empire Hudson* of convoy SC42 on 10 September by *U82* (Kptlt Siegfried Rollmann). By this time some 50 aircraft catapults had been ordered and the inviting new silhouette had become a startling feature in many convoys.

SC42 was still under attack from the *Markgraf* group up to 12 September 1942, when some boats were forced to break off due to a shortage of fuel. This made it necessary to reshuffle the remainder to close up gaps and then the shorter patrol line continued the search, but this time was severely hampered by natural radio interference and thick fog. As a result, only very few boats made contact with the next convoy to be found, SC44, and the pack was disbanded on 26 September because there were too few boats left in the western Atlantic. The remaining commanders were first given a free hand to do what they liked, but a short time later the four remaining near the Canadian coast were ordered to reconnoitre Belle Isle Strait and then the Cape Race area off the north and south of Newfoundland respectively. One of these was *U109* under Kptlt Heinrich Bleichrodt with Wolfgang Hirschfeld as radio operator. Hirschfeld kept a private, secret diary, despite such action being prohibited and punishable by court martial, the only one by a U-boat non-commissioned officer which is known to exist. This incredible record was first published in German and has now been translated into English by Geoffrey Brooks, to give a most tantalising insight into the bitterly cold conditions experienced in these hostile waters. Hirschfeld describes the low morale in the boat and concludes with the words: 'We are now the *Mordbrenner* group, with *Schlagetot* (Strike Dead) and *Reisswolf* (Tear to Shreds Wolf) towards the east, but there is nothing to strike or to tear at.'

The next wave of action was hardly under way when the Supreme Naval Command instructed Dönitz to send a wave of six boats into the Mediterranean. Such a move had been proposed as early as April 1941, but Dönitz's stubborn character impressed Hitler to such an extent that he sided with the U-boat Command and agreed to keep as many U-boats as possible in the all-important shipping lanes of the North Atlantic. However, by

Below: An aircraft has almost come to grief by rolling forwards and nearly falling off the front of the flight deck.

September it was obvious that Italian forces could not maintain the necessary back-up to protect ships running into North African ports and the need to keep Rommel's supply lines open became a most pressing task. This resulted in boats being withdrawn from the convoy routes. Some of them were sent to Spain for secret refuelling before making the perilous passage through the heavily guarded Strait of Gibraltar. This sequence actually presented Britain with an intriguing dilemma. Although Bletchley Park informed the Admiralty in London about this move into neutral Spanish waters, there was nothing which could be done about it without compromising the fact that Britain was reading the secret radio code. Therefore, the majority of boats had to be left in peace, to be attacked later when they tried negotiating the narrow Strait of Gibraltar.

The second fast moving patrol line also met an abundance of problems such as fog and strong natural radio interference so that many of the attacks were frustrated at the last minute. This was an especially bitter pill because convoy ON28, heading west to North America, was sighted by *U74* (Kptlt Eitel-Friedrich Kentrat) some 300 miles west of Ireland and then pursued for 800 nautical miles (almost 1,500km) without any success. The failures were put down to the natural conditions as well as the convoy's high speed of just over 10 knots making it impossible for U-boats to get close enough. This is not to say that every such attack ended in total failure. A number of U-boats did get close enough to SC48 to sink 11 merchant ships and two escorts. Yet, this small success could not conceal the fact that the overall sinking rate had dropped to another dramatic low.

The British Anti-Submarine Reports stated that, during October 1941, the enemy's effort had increased fivefold over the same period a year earlier, but the achievements were nowhere near equal to the exertions. British shipping losses, although still higher than during the previous summer, had fallen from the high total of the previous month. The argument that this was caused by poor weather cannot be substantiated because the weather of the previous year had been similar when the losses rose to an all-time high. Things looked most promising from the British point of view, as October started with no ships being sunk in convoy during the first two weeks, but then the eastbound convoy SC48 ran into the teeth of a wolf pack while some 400 miles south of Iceland, before it was met by the mid-ocean escort group. Since it was protected by only four escorts there were plenty of opportunities for the attacking pack, though radar put paid to a good number of attempts.

On 17 October *U568* (Kptlt Georg Preuss) started a delicate international incident by torpedoing the United States destroyer *Kearny* and killing a number of her crew. The *Kearny* managed to reach Iceland under its own steam, but the repercussions reverberated as far as Berlin, where Hitler imposed even tighter restrictions on U-boats shooting at supposedly neutral warships. During his later interrogation, Preuss defended himself by pointing out that it was impossible to distinguish the nationality of a blacked out destroyer protecting a convoy at night unless that ship made some effort to identify itself. In any case, he argued, what was a neutral doing in a hostile convoy? Although everybody in Germany agreed with him, it was still paramount to avoid the sabre-rattling efforts by warmongering politicians in the United States, to prevent the most powerful nation on earth from finding an excuse for joining the conflict against Germany. Preuss's attack was considered important because it followed only a few weeks after the so-called *Greer* incident when Hitler ordered that U-boats must not shoot at United States ships, even if they were attacked by them.

There are some dramatic charts on display in the museum at Bletchley Park showing the positions of wolf packs at this time and the desperate twists and turns taken by convoys to avoid them. Usually it was only when a patrol line extended beyond the range of the merchant ships that the convoys stumbled upon the extremities of the outside wing of the pack and came under attack. The weak link in the German system was that the decoded positions of the wolf packs were used so that merchant ships could be rerouted away from the potential hot spots.

All Dönitz could do was to react to the ever-hardening position at sea and come up with the same conclusions as before about possible reasons why U-boats were failing so miserably. He often remarked that 'coincidence always seems to favour the enemy' and more than once suggested that the cause could lie in the radio code. This idea also occurred to me in the mid-1960s, shortly after I started serious research into U-boats. Mentioning this theory to Kapitän zur See ausser Dienst (KptzSaD [aD=retired]) Otto Köhler (*U377*, communications expert and Commander of the Acoustic Torpedo School) and other ex-commanders of U-boats produced such strong statements that it was impossible to break into the code, even if the enemy had captured an Enigma machine set up for the day, that I abandoned this line of enquiry. Everybody assured me that it was folly even to consider such a possibility. It was made clear that the German naval code was too complicated and impossible to penetrate. This at least helped me to understand the strong terms in which the Supreme Naval Command told Dönitz that there was just no way that the codes were being compromised. There had to be another, far simpler solution. Dönitz didn't believe his superiors, but still stumbled on as before, making one of the biggest mistakes of the war. Later, on 1 February 1942, when a new four-wheel Enigma machine was introduced, this happened at a time when the general parameters of the war had changed so dramatically that no one in Germany noticed the effects of the resulting blackout at Bletchley Park.

Dönitz's view that coincidence always favoured the opposition was further supported by an incident towards the end of October 1941, when a number of boats sailed simultaneously from the French Atlantic bases. They were still heading west in the Bay of Biscay, when the B-Dienst provided evidence of a southward bound convoy on their very doorstep. Taking full advantage of the situation, the pack was ordered into a patrol line, while no fewer than six aircraft were sent out to help bring them to battle. Yet, despite this hive of activity so close to the German bases, nothing was sighted and the hunt was abandoned five days later. Dönitz realised that the expected reversal of fortune had not taken place. Once again, he had been outwitted by a smarter enemy and, to make matters even more demoralising, there was no way of even finding out how it was done. Having no alternative, the boats were ordered north-west into the old hunting ground between Britain and North America, while the U-boat Command brooded over its depressing failure. Germany was obviously incapable of bringing even the easiest of potential targets to battle, leaving Dönitz with the bitter pill that his wolf packs did not bring in the success he had expected.

Still not knowing how to handle the situation nor having any other clear option, Dönitz tinkered with the basic set-up, to abandon the fast patrol line concept in favour of several loose formations across the Atlantic. The vision of a large wolf pack bringing in any form of success had to be abandoned. These new, loose formations had just been conceived on paper and the necessary radio messages formulated when the Supreme Naval Command threw a spanner into the works by ordering Dönitz to employ every available boat off Gibraltar. This meant that he was left with no choice other than to evacuate the shipping lanes between Britain and America. Even a number of boats, which had just arrived off Newfoundland with explicit orders to attack shipping in the main anchorages there, had to be recalled. They had crossed the Atlantic for nothing. The situation in the U-boat Command must have been desperate. Dönitz, now holding the rank of Vizeadmiral, was comparatively low in the pecking order within the naval hierarchy and he didn't have any evidence of successes to help him push through his plans for the employment of submarines. Yet, despite having reached the lowest ebb of the war so far, he had the strength of character not to show his fears about the depressing conditions to his men.

When looking at the move to the Gibraltar area in more detail, it must be remembered that the first crisis occurred towards mid-November, when Britain realised that another group of U-boats was attempting to enter the Mediterranean. The best way for the British forces to prevent U-boats interfering with their Mediterranean operations was to plug the narrow gap between Cape Trafalgar near Gibraltar and Cape Spartel in North Africa. However, the news of the threatened break-in appeared such a short time before the event that it was impossible for the Royal Navy to organise effective counter-measures. As a stopgap action, HMS *Stork* was ordered to organise an endless patrol chain with two other destroyers and three corvettes at 08.00 hours on 27 November 1941. Things had to move so fast that the ships went to sea without their usual pre-sailing conference. Instead they merely came alongside HMS *Stork* to receive instructions.

The distance between the two capes was a trifle over 42 nautical miles (almost 80 kilometres), making it impractical to position a stationary chain of ships. Instead each ship was told to keep on the move with a maximum speed of 13 knots. While these orders were being issued, someone calculated that the effective distance between ships under such conditions should be 6,720 metres, meaning 12 would be required to plug the gap. One theoretical problem with such a plan was that ships could not be positioned, like U-boats, at the limit of their lookout's vision because some of them would be bound to drop out sooner or later in order to explore a contact, meaning that large gaps would be created in the chain. The intention was to keep these open until the ship returned to its position, rather than close up because that could lead to even more confusion further along the line. An additional problem was that the top speed of a corvette was only a few knots more than the cruising speed of the chain, so closing the gap could indeed pose a major problem. These desperate measures had to be taken to meet such a deeply worrying threat.

The first group of U-boats had already passed into the Mediterranean, therefore the Royal Navy had some knowledge of the havoc U-boats were likely to wreak there and made it difficult for the next wave to get in. *U202* (Kptlt Günter Poser), *U432* (Kptlt Heinz-Otto Schultze), *U558* (Kptlt Günther Krech), and *U569* (Kptlt Hans-Peter Hinsch) returned to their Biscay ports as a result of having sustained heavy damage. Five other boats, *U95* (Gerd Schreiber), *U206* (Kptlt Herbert Opitz), *U208* (ObLtzS Alfred Schlieper), *U433* (Kptlt Hans Ey) and *U451* (Korvkpt Eberhard Hoffmann) were sunk while on their way into the Mediterranean.

At about the same time as various U-boats were trying to break into the Mediterranean, the boats moved from the Atlantic were ready to pounce on convoys to the west of Gibraltar. But, forewarned by Bletchley Park, the British deployed 233 Squadron RAF with Hudsons, and the Fleet Air Arm provided a number of Swordfish aircraft, to be ready to greet the newly arriving opposition. The British commanders also had advance warning about a possible air raid on Gibraltar and therefore ordered convoy HG76 to sail a day early, during the afternoon of 14 December. Four tankers and one freighter left at about the same time, to sail to the Middle East around the southern tip of Africa. Bletchley Park was able to produce the stunning information that there were no U-boats trying to break into the Mediterranean at that critical moment. This made it possible to withdraw the guard ships from the Strait of Gibraltar to help the struggling convoys. In all, convoy HG76 consisted of 32 ships in nine columns, travelling at 7.3 knots and protected by 16 escorts and the escort carrier *Audacity*. Five more escorts joined the group later, but four were subsequently forced to withdraw. On this occasion there were only four aircraft available and experience had shown that even such a small number was likely to be reduced very rapidly once action started. To make matters worse, such action did not have to involve the Germans; the Atlantic itself threw up enough unfavourable weather to damage aircraft. This was so bad that flying was kept to an absolute minimum, with aircraft being launched only when U-boats were known to be in vicinity.

The first air attack did not fall to *Audacity*'s aircraft at all, but to a Swordfish without a radio. Therefore, there was no way of warning the convoy of the approaching U-boat. However, men aboard HMS *Stork* heard three depth charges explode, making them dash off to explore the intrusion. Unfortunately it took almost half an hour to reach the spot and by that time the sea was empty, leaving no alternative other than to conduct a prolonged asdic search with HMS *Deptford* and HMS *Rhododendron*. It didn't take long for the U-boat Command to realise that they were faced with a strongly protected convoy, but Dönitz argued that the majority of crews and commanders were experienced enough to cope and therefore every effort was made to find the merchant ships. This was not easy since long-range Focke-Wulf reconnaissance aircraft failed to find any trace of the merchant ships, which seemed to vanish immediately after every sighting report from a U-boat. It was a case of spotting the convoy, being put down and then surfacing again onto empty seas. Later when the heavy and highly unmanoeuvrable Kondors did sight the convoy, they came under immediate attack from fighters from *Audacity*, but as luck would have it, the guns on two aircraft jammed at the critical moment, allowing the Germans to make a hurried getaway. Both crews reached France, to emphasise the fact that these reconnaissance aircraft were no match for nimble fighters and an alternative way of keeping convoys under surveillance must be found if large and clumsy aircraft were going to play a greater role in future battles.

Losing sight of the convoy, finding it again, attacks and counter-attacks became the order of the next few days. This action can best be summed up by a signal sent from HMS *Stork* at 05.28 hours on 20 December 1940, after a hectic night, 'HMS *Stanley* sunk by a U-boat. The U-boat sunk by HMS *Stork*.' The Admiralty made a concerted effort to unravel the events after they had come to an end on 23 December 1941, but only came up with the statement that it was impossible to determine the various movements. However, the Commander-in-Chief of the Western Approaches did remark that it was most surprising that more attacks were not carried out against HG76. The gloom that followed at the U-boat Command is hard to describe. This bitter battle had resulted in the sinking of the *Audacity*, the *Stanley* and three merchant ships but even the valuable carrier did not compensate Germany for the loss of five U-boats. Dönitz came up with a famous remark that the presence of aircraft made the chances of being sunk greater than any prospects of success.

Top: A Swordfish aircraft has skidded over the flight deck of the escort carrier HMS *Chaser* rather than being arrested by the braking wire. Planes with open cockpits, like this one, were used at sea until the end of the war.

Above: A more modern Seafire crashing on HMS *Chaser*, killing the pilot and destroying the plane. Taking off and landing on carriers was a major problem, especially as the majority of aircraft had not been designed for coping with short, slippery, pitching and rolling flight decks. A high proportion of pilots lacked the experience to cope with such demanding precision flying.

Left: KptIt Otto Salman of *U52* in Lorient. A photograph such as this might easily be regarded as him being greeted by just another onlooker. After all, the person on the left hardly looks impressive, yet he is a most interesting character who might not be associated with U-boat bases. It is Field Marshal Erwin Rommel, the Desert Fox, who became famous as commander of the Afrika Korps.

Chapter 10

The First Thrust Against the United States December 1941–February 1942

On 7 December 1941, Japan struck a devastating blow against the United States by attacking its Pacific naval base at Pearl Harbor near Honolulu on the Hawaiian Islands, halfway between America and Asia. This left Hitler with little political alternative other than to declare war on the United States as well, thus changing the parameters of World War 2 out of all proportions. It certainly left a good number in the German Navy flabbergasted, wondering whether there would be any point in continuing the struggle. Such feelings had already surfaced during the early summer of 1941, when Germany declared war on Russia. Now it felt even worse. The bulk of the German Army was suffering on the cold wastes of the steppes and in addition there were troops positioned from the North Cape of Norway as far south as the fringes of the Sahara. The fact that Japan had taken a little pressure off the back door in the faraway Pacific was easily cancelled out by the most powerful nation on earth joining the war as another adversary.

Today it is well known that Germany planned on launching its attack against the United States with half a dozen U-boats, but one of them remained in dock for repairs, so only five actually sailed. Yet, astonishing as it was, this minute force inflicted incredibly heavy casualties, so serious that much of the operation was hushed up after the war. Another, far crueller, step to prevent people from asking too many awkward questions was to label the merchant mariners, who sailed oil tankers along the front line of America's east coast, as 'draft dodgers'. After the war they were excluded from being given the recognition of veteran status. It was not until after a tireless struggle by Ian Millar and The Sons and Daughters of the US Merchant Marine that this was belatedly bestowed a few years before the end of the turbulent 20th century.

Although the first onslaught against the United States went under the imposing name of Operation *Paukenschlag* ('a roll on the kettledrums'), it was not a wolf pack operation. The name came about during a discussion with Hitler, when the possibility of America entering the war was brought up. Dönitz asked to be given ample warning of such a move so that he could be ready to strike a powerful blow, using the German expression for a sudden impact 'on the kettledrums', and this term was later adopted as the code word. Some weeks later, shortly after the attack on Pearl Harbor, he looked less enthusiastically upon such action, saying it would almost certainly turn into a suicide mission from which he did not expect anyone to return. Although this may sound highly dramatic today, it must be borne in mind that U-boats had already been driven out of British coastal waters, the Bay of Biscay was becoming a death trap, and December 1941, when these plans were being formulated, was the worst month for U-boat losses so far. Even the vast open spaces of the endless Atlantic did not provide enough hiding places for the grey wolves and the majority of boats which found the enemy were driven mercilessly away, often nursing vicious wounds while repairing serious damage. The war had been only a few months old when old lags, such as Günther Prien, Herbert Schultze and Otto

Kretschmer told Dönitz that the coastal waters around the British Isles were too dangerous. Retribution was too quick in coming and therefore it was not worth taking the risk of seeking out shipping close to land.

Now, after two years of war, Dönitz was ordering his commanders to go against this advice, although he guessed that this new land, on the far side of the Atlantic, was likely to throw up even worse conditions than those experienced in British waters towards the beginning of the war. Everybody was likely to be fully prepared and therefore ready and waiting for the U-boats to strike. In addition to this, it was a case of hitting shipping routes running parallel with the shore, where the main channels could be seen from land, so that airfields, harbours and other lairs of retribution were uncomfortably close. Yet, despite these problems, the U-boat Command felt there was no alternative other than for U-boats to do their bit by striking at any soft underbellies still left exposed. The big hurdle was that no one could foretell where those vulnerable spots were likely to be. Britain had reorganised its merchant shipping routes before the war started, withdrawing vulnerable traffic from the obvious hot spots and now it looked highly likely that the United States was going to do the same. Therefore, Dönitz had to count on his U-boats facing long journeys only to come home empty handed with considerable damage, if they made it back at all. In view of this, any strike in the far western Atlantic would have to be carefully co-ordinated so that one boat didn't run into a trap set for another. Therefore, it was planned that all five boats should start their operations at exactly the same time, on 13 January 1942, in order to lessen the effects of any retribution.

Yet, when the crews reached America, they couldn't believe their eyes. Coastal towns were illuminated, ships sailed with navigation lights and the local radio even announced the departure times. Instead of heavy opposition, U-boats faced a free-for-all bonanza, which they called their 'Second Happy Time' or 'Second Golden Time'. Targets were so fast and furious in coming that there was no need for any co-ordinated group action. It was merely a case of crossing the Atlantic, disposing of torpedoes and returning with an abundance of success pennants fluttering from the extended periscope. What was more, the first boats of the second wave, consisting of *U103* (Kptlt Werner Winter), *U106* (Kptlt Hermann Rasch) and *U107* (Kptlt Harald Gelhaus), arrived in the area between Cape Breton Island on Nova Scotia and Cape Hatteras in North Carolina while the first boats were still active, turning the seas into flaming infernos. The United States did not have a pipeline running north and therefore a variety of oils and petrol were carried along the coast by a virtually endless chain of tankers, and the seaside communities along their route did not wish to lose their potential summer visitors by declaring a state of emergency. Therefore, illuminations were kept on, while people watched the massacre from land. The traffic between Cape Hatteras and New York turned out to be so dense that the boats ran out of torpedoes before they could tackle all the easily

Left: This probably shows *U66* (ObLtzS Gerhard Seehausen) sinking. It was an ocean-going boat of Type IXC used for long-range operations to America and into the South Atlantic. The wide upper deck was a characteristic feature. This type was double-hulled which meant that a number of tanks were wrapped around the outside of the pressure hull to make this extra width possible.

available targets. Although U-boats maintained radio silence, even after their first attacks, the Operations Room in Kernével near Lorient realised what was going on from the sudden increase in SOS calls. Only a fraction of these used the SSS distress call, introduced by the British authorities after the start of the war to identify an attack by submarine.

Once again, this stage of the war has been disfigured by historians, who have given a misleading image of what was going on by concentrating on Operation *Paukenschlag*. Far more important in the mind of the U-boat Command at the time were the heavy losses sustained during December, the bloody battles to the west of Gibraltar, heavy action in the Mediterranean and a group of boats up in the desolate polar seas. All this was taking place against a backdrop of bitter differences with the Supreme Naval Command. Dönitz was trying to tell them that U-boats should be employed in areas where they could sink the largest number of ships, not in already evacuated shipping lanes of the bitter north. This squabble was made even worse by one of Hitler's unexpected hunches, suggesting that an Allied invasion of Norway was imminent. Thus, a few days after *U123* (Kptlt Reinhard Hardegen) started the offensive in the western Atlantic by sinking the 8,998grt freighter *Cyclops* (Cpt William Holden), Hitler ordered the large surface units in France to return home and a number of U-boats to take up positions along the Norwegian coast. Although detailed interference by Hitler in naval matters was rare, he did on this occasion go against the wishes of the Supreme Naval Command and order the battleships to sail along the European coast — the now famous Channel Dash.

The general situation at home regarding the availability of U-boats was not good at all. In fact Germany started its attack against the United States with fewer boats fully operational boats than at the beginning of the war. Despite records showing that 37 were at sea, only 18 were in a position to strike. The others were either on their way home or on their way out. To make matters worse, 54 were held up in port, awaiting repairs. This appalling state of affairs had already been brought to the attention of the Supreme Naval Command in appropriately stiff language by Dönitz, saying that it was more than pointless to call up skilled workers from shipyards for service with the armed forces, when they could be contributing far more to the war effort by remaining in their jobs. This imprudent call-up even created havoc with essential paperwork. Many of the shipyards had offices scattered over quite a large area, often on several sites, and shuffling the necessary papers from one to another slowed to such an extent that there were times when the internal mail system came to a complete standstill merely because the main messenger, who knew where all the offices were, suddenly left without a great deal of notice, and his successor had no clue as to where documents should be going. U-boat Command officers had just laid these depressing figures on Dönitz's desk when KptzS Hans-Georg von Friedeburg (head of the Organisation Department) came up with the most unwelcome news that the situation regarding skilled workers in the shipyards was now so bad that he could no longer forecast the number of new boats coming to the front because too many production lines were lying idle.

The year 1942 was only a few days old when the Supreme Naval Command lost interest in its direct control of U-boat operations and handed much of the command back to Dönitz. (Actually, he had never lost that position but now no longer had to work under direct orders from Berlin.) His immediate reaction was to divert boats heading south, towards the Azores, into the far western reaches of the convoy routes between America and Britain. His argument was that it was best to strike where traffic was likely to be densest and where the opposition was likely to be weakest. Yet, the assumption that Canada was as reticent as the United States proved to be wrong. The thrust into the waters off Newfoundland by Type VII boats of the *Ziethen* group turned out to be another disappointing failure. Fog, blinding snowstorms and intense cold combined with exceptionally heavy seas meant that individual sinkings were low, with the majority managing to find only a couple of targets, while one boat, *U84* (Kptlt Horst Uphoff), came back empty handed.

Much of this action took place relatively close to the shore, meaning retribution was always quick in coming, making life exceptionally uncomfortable on top of the difficulties thrown up by the natural elements. The most dangerous threat came from iced up vents making it impossible to dive at times and forcing U-boats to submerge every two to three hours to thaw out the problem. Such ice interference had already occurred in the Baltic and in the Arctic, but not while aggressive military forces were also at play. The only feasible remedy was to lower the boat into the slightly warmer water just under the surface and then to move at speed to thaw the offending solid obstructions in the ports. This, of course, resulted in the interior filling with considerable volumes of water of 10 tons or more, making it necessary to run all available ballast pumps at full power to remove it again before attempting to dive. Whilst this was uncomfortable at the best of times, it was suicidal if there was military opposition around. Several commanders overcame the threat by using their authority to withdraw further south without informing the U-boat Command. This actually turned out to be quite a plus point when such long voyages made it evident that the official performance figures were somewhat inaccurate and that fuel could be consumed much more slowly than anticipated.

This news later induced Dönitz to send the smaller Type VII boats to the United States and to take a considerable additional risk by sending *UA* (Korvkpt Hans Cohausz) behind them as supply boat. Up to now it had been the usual practice to refuel U-boats after their outward voyage, before their position had been revealed by aggressive action, so that they were in a good position to return independently, without having to seek further help if pursued by enemy forces. However, because opposition in the Cape Hatteras area was nonexistent, Dönitz decided to send in some smaller boats and then refuel them after the action. This worked exceedingly well and will be dealt with in a later chapter.

Moving Type VII boats to American waters did not go ahead without inflicting enormous additional discomforts on the crew and expecting them to take some additional risks. First, every available tank was filled with fuel including some washing water tanks. Trimming tanks, torpedo compensating tanks and diving tanks were also filled with the thick diesel oil. In theory, this would be consumed first and then replaced by seawater by the time the tanks were needed for action, but there was always a risk of remnants of thick oil being ejected during venting to leave a noticeable trail on the surface for a potential hunter to home in on. In addition to having fuel cramped into every available space, commanders were told to take the shortest possible route along the great circle, to avoid struggling against tidal streams, and to ride out storms submerged, rather than battle against raging seas and wind. All this actually worked and gave each boat an additional 14 to 20 days in the operations area. However, the supreme sacrifice made by the crews has hardly been recognised.

Operation *Paukenschlag* had just been launched when Dönitz

planned another thrust further south into the Caribbean, with a view to attacking tankers and allied refuelling stations. Intelligence gathered through neutral sources had indicated that such a move had already been anticipated because the stations used by merchant traffic running down to the deep south of America were being fitted with floating booms across the entrances. Rather than put the U-boat Command off, this suggested that rich targets were to be had around Port of Spain, Aruba and Curaçao. New Type IX boats in Germany were hurriedly made ready for a fast passage to France where they were fully fuelled and kitted out with the necessary tropical gear. This whole operation may sound like a romantic adventure, but it taxed the crews beyond their wildest imagination, with temperatures often rising to that of a moderate baking oven and the bulkheads as well as virtually everything else inside being constantly and most unpleasantly damp or even soaking wet from condensation. Although a rich harvest was reaped, this did not go without a number of tantalising disasters. Shelling oil installations on land was part of the plan and at least one boat, *U156* (Korvkpt Werner Hartenstein, later of *Laconia* fame), tried this without removing the watertight tampion from the end of the barrel, thus seriously injuring a couple of men who were later landed on Martinique for hospital treatment

Top and above: UA, with its unique conning tower, being used as supply boat in the North Atlantic. This was the only U-boat which had such a characteristic fairing around the large deck gun. Built originally for Turkey as *Batiray*, the war started before it could be delivered and this huge ocean-going boat was commissioned into the Kriegsmarine to serve in a variety of functions until it was relegated to the training flotillas in April 1942.

Chapter 11
The Sea Wolves

Above: U735 being commissioned by ObLtzS Hans-Joachim Börner on 28 December 1942, a black period for U-boats when an above average number were sunk.

Above: U135 ploughing its way through heavy seas with water pouring out of the vents. The space between the upper deck and pressure hull was designed to fill with water when the boat dived and in rough weather the sea continued to gurgle its way through this space.

Left: Loading one of the bow torpedoes. The loading ramp and derrick for lowering the 1½-ton weapon was removed before the boat went to sea.

Below left: U436 under Kptlt Günther Seibicke reloading a bow torpedo on the high seas. Type VII boats carried two, and Type IX boats four torpedoes in external containers from which they could not be fired. This meant that the heavy 'eels' had to be brought below before they could be used. Doing this in warm climates was quite refreshing at times, but imagine having to perform such a task during a cold northern winter. The loading gear was heavy and assembling it in mid-ocean was not easy.

Below right: U564 partly submerged to make the handling of the torpedo easier. Once again, this was quite refreshing in warm southern waters, but many men had to do this in bitterly cold conditions.

Right: Obergefreiter Karl Hornenbroich (left) and Technischerobergefreiter Hans Bauer wearing light denim jackets aboard *U48*. Hornenbroich is always seen smiling, even after having fallen into the drink.

Below left: LtzS Clemens Schöler as 1WO of *U564*, before becoming a commander, demonstrating why the coats issued to men of the seaman's division were fitted with large lapels.

Below right: Obergefreiter Noack of *U123* wearing a sheepskin jacket without lapels, indicating that he was a member of the mechanical division. Lapels got in the way when working in the close confines of the engine room.

Above: The duty watch aboard *U29*. Commanders were left very much to their own devices to decide how they organised duty rotas. Many allowed the lookouts to talk and smoke, taking the view that they would be far more alert when comfortable and relaxed. However, some commanders were sticklers for rules and kept their men on unnecessarily tight apron strings.

Above: ObLtzS Georg Lassen (*U29* and *U160*) and (left) Kptlt Otto Schuhart (*U25* and *U29*) in April 1940 when Lassen was 1WO aboard *U29*, the boat which sank the aircraft carrier *Courageous* in the Western Approaches shortly after the outbreak of war.

Left: Kptlt Engelbert Endrass in Lorient, sporting the Knight's Cross with Oakleaves around the neck. He served as 1WO aboard *U47* when Günther Prien penetrated the Royal Navy's anchorage at Scapa Flow to sink the battleship *Royal Oak* and later he became commander of *U46*.

Right: From left to right: Hans Stock (*U659*), Heinrich Lehmann-Willenbrock (Flotilla Leader), Hanns-Ferdinand Massmann (*U137*), Konstantin von Puttkamer (*U46*) and Horst Höltring (*U604*).

Below left: Wolfgang Lüth (right, *U138*, *U43*, *U181* and flotilla leader) was one of only two U-boat commanders who were awarded the Knight's Cross with Oakleaves, Swords and Diamonds.

Below right: Kptlt Erich Würdemann as commander of *U506* before he was awarded the Knight's Cross.

Left: Kptlt Heinrich 'Ajax' Bleichrodt, photographed when commanding *U48*.

Below: Kptlt Otto Schuhart on top of the conning tower of *U29*.

Right: Korvkpt Erich Topp, commander of the famous 'Red Devil' boat, while serving with the 7th U-Flotilla in St Nazaire, wearing a white summer uniform jacket.

Below: Kptlt Engelbert Endrass as commander of *U46* wearing a standard issue leather coat.

Below right: Obermaschinist Lücking of *U103*.

Above: Korvkpt Wilhelm Dommes of *U178* on the left with his First Watch Officer, Wilhelm Spahr, in the Indian Ocean.

Left: Wilhelm Spahr had a most colourful career, having served as Obersteuermann of *U47* during the famous Scapa Flow raid. Following this he was made an officer and eventually brought *U178* back from the Far East as commander.

Right: Looking at the emblem of the black cat ('3x') on the conning tower one might assume that this is *U48,* but the bunker in the background was built after the most successful boat of the war had left France, so it seems highly likely that this is *U564,* commanded by Teddy Suhren, the one-time 1WO of *U48.* In the foreground is an 88mm deck gun. The intake of the radio aerial can be seen by the cat's feet, while the fog horn or typhoon is visible below the spray deflector.

Below: U48, a Type VIIB, the most successful U-boat of World War 2.

Left:
U86 under Kptlt Walter Schug, wearing the white cap on the left. The men are wearing their own boat's emblem on the side of their caps. The torpedo sight, without the binoculars clipped on top, can be seen in the foreground.

Left: Men of *U165* (Kptlt Eberhard Hoffmann) going through their drill with the 105mm quick-firing deck gun.

Above: U251 painted white while stationed in northern Norway.

Above right: The torpedo sight in action. At first it was necessary to aim the entire boat at the target, but later the sights could be rotated by turning the notched wheel which the man is holding and the deflection angle was transmitted to the torpedoes lying in the tubes.

Above: U10 in the Baltic with the binoculars clipped on top of the torpedo sight.

Above: U527 (Kptlt Herbert Uhlig) at gun practice. This was a Type IXC, therefore the gun had a calibre of 105mm. The men are wearing safety harnesses with clips for attaching themselves to the boat in rough weather.

Above:
U30 with the old style of conning tower design.

Left: U73 in St Nazaire, showing the early type of conning tower.

Right: LtzS Horst Bredow as Second Watch Officer of *U288* under ObLtzS Willy Meyer shortly before an injury forced him into hospital and the boat went out without him, never to return. Horst Bredow is the founder and the director of the now famous U-Boot-Archiv.

Below: U415 on its third operational voyage under Kptlt Kurt Neide, shortly before ObLtzS Herbert Werner, author of the book *Iron Coffins*, took over.

Chapter 12
Supply Submarines and the First Self–Contained Wolf Pack March–June 1942

Supply ships were one of the last types to be developed by the Kriegsmarine, despite them having been high on the list of priorities during World War 1 and their importance being further elevated by postwar evaluations. One of the reasons was that they were classed as men-of-war and therefore had to be included in the figures of the Anglo-German Naval Agreement, which restricted the size of the German fleet to approximately one third of the British navy. The few purpose-built supply ships available at the outbreak of World War 2, such as *Westerwald* and the famous *Altmark*, formed an integral part of the commerce raiding programme by supporting pocket battleships. From the beam these ships looked very much like any other modern tanker of the period, but when flying directly overhead it was possible to see that they possessed the sleek and slender lines of a warship, rather than the more bulbous shape of a merchantman. This cigar shape was further pronounced at the waterline to give them the high speed needed to keep up with their fast charges. Emergency mobilisation plans for converting a variety of merchant ships to serve naval purposes were in hand when the war started and were even practised long before

Hitler came to power. The first trial of using a merchantman to support a warship took place as early as 1928, when the tanker *Hansa* from Atlantik Tank Reederei escorted the light cruiser *Emden* (KptzS Richard Foster) on a world cruise. At that time, it was argued that any large scale conflict with a strong sea power was likely to confine the majority of German merchant ships in port; therefore, it would not be much of an economic sacrifice if that shipping was engaged in military activities.

Seven different categories of supply ship, ranging from small coastal oilers to long-distance ocean-going tankers, were created shortly after the outbreak of war. This programme, together with

Below: It is possible that this is *U564* under Kptlt Reinhard Suhren, but it could also be that the other boat, just visible behind the signalman's right leg, is *U564*. Whatever, it shows lookouts faithfully sweeping the seas and sky in their sectors while an attempt is being made to contact the other boat so that provisions can be passed from one to the other. The cone-shaped device on top of the torpedo aimer, to the left of what could be the commander, is a loudhailer. Being so close together on the high seas put the boats into such vulnerable positions that the use of radios was prohibited for two days either side of a scheduled meeting.

the employment of the vessels, ran relatively smoothly until the early summer of 1941, when British forces sank nine of the 10 supply ships for the battleship *Bismarck*, as we have seen, bringing refuelling activities in far-off waters to an abrupt halt. Up to that time, U-boats had made use of supply ships for surface units by employing their facilities to extend the range of a few individually operating long-distance submarines. Some U-boats also escorted auxiliary cruisers through the turbulent waters of the North Atlantic and were rewarded with plentiful supplies to give them the opportunity of hitting at some far-distant locations before returning home. In addition to this, there had been several occasions where homeward-bound boats passed spare fuel, remaining torpedoes and left-over food to outward-going colleagues. Therefore, the process of moving goods from one boat to another had been practised to a small extent and the U-boat Command was well aware of the problems faced by such operations. The biggest of these was that inflatable dinghies carried by U-boats were hardly suitable for

carrying heavy, often sharp-edged goods, and the fire hoses were usually neither long nor thick enough to transfer fuel comfortably from one boat to another. Yet, these difficulties, incurred during unplanned meetings, were minor snags and could easily be ironed out with a little foresight and preparation.

The disastrous losses around the *Bismarck* campaign may have dampened German enthusiasm by making it quite plain that the North Atlantic had become a no-go area for surface ships, but those turbulent waters were also swept by the most inhospitable weather with plenty of opportunities for slipping through to unfrequented parts of more distant regions. So, during the early autumn of 1941, another attempt was made for U-boats to operate with surface supply ships. This time a wolf pack was sent into the South Atlantic to be first refuelled from the legendary auxiliary cruiser *Atlantis* under KptzS Bernhard Rogge. It would appear that only one strong character voiced any noteworthy opposition to the scheme. This was KptzS Kurt Weyher, who had earlier commanded the raider *Orion*. He made it quite plain to the Supreme Naval Command that *Atlantis* had already broken a world record by having remained at sea for the longest period of time ever and that it was unfair to burden such a crew with the arduous task of refuelling submarines. They should be given permission to return home. Although Bletchley Park never cracked the raider code, the cryptanalysts could read the U-boat messages and thereby work out the position of the meeting points in lonely parts of the ocean. As a result, *Atlantis* was sunk on 22 November 1941, her 622nd day at sea, by the British heavy cruiser *Devonshire* and all the South Atlantic wolf pack could do was to pick up survivors.

Atlantis's role in helping U-boats was very much a stopgap measure until a properly kitted out submarine supply ship could be got to sea. The preparations for this were so thorough that two identical ships were assembled in France. The idea was that the freighter *Cap Hadid*, with special modifications to look like the submarine supply ship *Python*, could slip into *Python's* berth during the hours of darkness, and, it was hoped, fool any agents scouring the waterside for unusual movements. *Python* eventually sailed on 6 November 1941, carrying almost 100 torpedoes and a plentiful supply of ammunition for U-boat guns, as well as all the other necessities for keeping wolf packs in the southern oceans. Once again, Bletchley Park was one step ahead by reading the U-boat code and was, therefore, well aware that she had picked up survivors from *Atlantis* and was continuing with the main objective of her cruise. Thus, it was only a small matter of sending the *Dorsetshire* to sink her on 1 December 1941. Following this, Germany had to pull out every stop to bring survivors home. The few U-boats in southern waters could never have coped on their own, and many of the men owed their lives to support from several large Italian boats based in Bordeaux. At the same time these two sinkings slammed the door tightly shut on any further thoughts of using surface supply ships.

This entire concept was thrown into a totally new light during the following Sunday, when Japan launched its attack against Pearl Harbor. So far, most U-boats had been operating relatively close to the Biscay bases in France and only a few long-distance boats had ventured further afield. Now, suddenly, with America's entry into the war, it looked as if long voyages would become the order of the day. The snag was that no one dared even to think about sending more surface support ships to sea and it was going to be a while before the new submarine tankers would be available. Earlier, at the outbreak of war, Hitler saw no great urgency in building this type of craft and 14 months of conflict were allowed to pass before the first purpose-built Type XIV

Above: The massive, purpose-built Type XIV supply submarine, *U460*. The boat had two commanders: Korvkpt der Reserve Friedrich Schäfer and later Kptlt der Reserve Ebe Schnoor. This shows the wide deck with the rather puny 37mm quick-firing gun.

Above: The purpose-built submarine tanker *U461* supplying the 'Red Devil' boat, *U552*. It was standard practice to refuel with one ship being towed behind another, rather than sailing side by side.

supply tanker was laid down at the Germania Works in Kiel. Another year passed before this boat was finally commissioned on 15 November 1941 as *U459* by Kptlt Georg von Wilamowitz-Moellendorf, one of the oldest commanders, who had already seen service in U-boats during World War 1. Although called 'The Wild Moritz' behind his back, he was rather a placid broad-shouldered officer, who fitted far better into larger boats than the cramped conditions of ordinary submarines.

U459 was running through its first trials during a most momentous period of time when the U-boat Command was faced with another one of those frequent mechanical disasters. This time the problems hinged around the largest U-boat, the Type XB minelayer. The first of these had been commissioned on 26 July 1941 as *U116* by Korvkpt Werner von Schmidt. This first submarine minelayer to be built since World War 1, carried 66 special moored mines called SMA (Shaft Mine Type A). These were accommodated in free flooding vertical shafts and therefore had to be capable of withstanding high water pressure when the boat dived deep. Unfortunately the mines had a tendency to detonate too early, giving the U-boat crew severe headaches and, of course, like a match, they worked only once, rendering the whole process somewhat pointless. The submarine mines used in British coastal waters shortly after the beginning of the war were a different variety. Those were ejected through torpedo tubes and could therefore be deposited by any boat with the special mine modification if the commander had the necessary special training to use them. In the end, this torpedo type was used for the first mining operations against the United States. *U373* (Kptlt Paul-Karl Loeser) attacked Delaware Bay on 11 June 1942, sinking the tug *John R. Williams* and the following night *U87* (Kptlt Joachim Berger) laid mines off Boston, but nothing ran into them. *U373* was a standard Type VIIC, but *U87* is interesting

inasmuch that it was by far the last VIIB to be commissioned. It was laid down at the small Flenderwerft in Lübeck on 18 April 1940 and not commissioned until 19 August 1941.

This problem with the early detonations had still not been solved when the United States joined in the war and, since the massive Type XB was nearly ready to go to sea, it was decided to convert *U116* into a supply submarine as a stopgap measure to take advantage of the 'Second Golden Time' in American waters. Even this was going to take too long. Therefore, the U-boat Command had the choice of either abandoning plans of refuelling in the Western Atlantic or sacrificing a long-range front-line boat to act as tanker. As has been mentioned before, this thought was just formulating when it was realised that *UA* was coming to the end of its operational life. She had seen considerable action, having herself been refuelled several times from surface supply ships, but she was nowhere near as nifty as the similar sized Type IX boats. In addition to this, *UA* had suffered considerable damage during earlier depth charge attacks, meaning it was due to be withdrawn from active, front-line service anyway, making it an ideal choice for replenishing other boats in out-of-the-way locations of the western Atlantic.

UA's ninth and last operational cruise took her into the western Atlantic for the first experiments to replenish U-boats from a submarine tanker. However, these plans were frustrated by an ominous grinding noise in the engine room, less than a day after leaving Lorient. Finally it was 14 March 1942, after a delay of three weeks, before *UA* headed west under Korvkpt Hans Cohausz. The refuelling experiments went quite well, although pumping fuel through a relatively delicate pipe was no

easy matter and the men felt that they needed a better way of shutting the pump off when the hose snapped, otherwise a large conspicuous pool of floating oil could act as an easy giveaway for passing aircraft. This refuelling experiment was taking place just two months after the introduction of the fourth rotor in the naval Enigma machine, meaning Bletchley Park had been locked out, unable to read the German operational U-boat code. This meant that there was no way for Britain to discover the secret refuelling locations, and so *UA* and its three charges, *U203* (Kptlt Rolf Mützelburg), *U84* (Kptlt Horst Uphoff) and *U202* (Kptlt Hans-Heinz Linder) were left in peace to return with comparatively positive remarks about this first ever experiment to supply submarines from a submersible tanker. It is interesting to note that an Allied transit aircraft reported a supply ship to be refuelling three submarines some 400 miles to the east of St Paul Rocks on 19 April 1942. At the time this was put down to having been Italian boats, although a similar sighting report, by another aircraft, of a pack consisting of 25 U-boats, was disregarded as fantasy.

When these first refuellings from submarines took place, the war in the western Atlantic had been raging for the best part of two months and even the hard-headed Americans, who refused to take the U-boat threat seriously at first, realised that something had to be done about the disastrous losses on their own doorstep. Consequently, the finding of targets was becoming a notable problem and, on top of this, retaliation was determined enough not to let U-boats off scot-free anymore. All the U-boat Command knew was that, although refuelling experiments were successful, the overall results were more than disappointing.

The four submarines involved with this first experiment were at sea for a total of 200 days, during which eight ships were torpedoed. One of those, MV *Stanvac Melbourne*, was only damaged, to be sunk later by *U515* (Kptlt Werner Henke) and another ship, SS *Harry F. Sinclair*, also torpedoed by *U203*, was towed to Baltimore, where she was repaired to see further service. It would be all too easy to dismiss the U-boat crews as inexperienced dummies, but that was certainly not the case. *U203* was among the top 38 U-boats, *U202* was among the top 45 and both *UA* and *U84* were among the top 72 out of a total of 1,171 U-boats. Yet, their overall performance in American waters could hardly be said even to have kept pace with the war at sea. Eighteen months earlier, during the 'Happy Time' of autumn 1940, boats were at sea on average for just over two weeks and a good many of the ace commanders were back in port less than 10 days after leaving, having expended all their torpedoes in that short time. Now, each boat was away for almost two months and then came home with torpedoes still on board because fuel and food were running low.

The first purpose-built supply submarine, *U459*, was prepared so hastily that the U-boat Command decided to send her the longer distance direct from Germany, rather than replenish in France before commencing the two week long crossing of the Atlantic. Yet, even this plan was frustrated by mechanical trouble, meaning it was necessary to call at Heligoland before attempting the breakout. Eventually it was 29 March 1942 when *U459* followed *UA* west. However, this massive monster of a submarine could cope with more than just three charges and first refuelled a number of Type VII boats

Above left: Of course both boats had to come to a standstill, if solid goods needed to be transferred. This picture of the inflatable was taken from *U68* (Korvkpt Karl-Friedrich Merten) with the Italian *Pietro Calvi* in the background.

Left: Men aboard *UA* preparing hoses to provide a Type VIIC with fuel in mid-Atlantic.

which had previously been dispatched to American waters when it was realised there was little opposition. We have already seen that Dönitz took the big risk of engaging these first and refuelling them afterwards. There had been so little retaliation from the Americans that Dönitz and his staff thought it was a gamble worth taking. *U571* (Kptlt Helmut Möhlmann), *U572* (Kptlt Heinz Hirsacker) and *U582* (Kptlt Werner Schulte), which had been engaged against convoys SC125, ON176 and ONS2, were first provided with enough fuel to get home. Then *U459* moved further south to feed another 12 boats bound for the southern United States coast or the Caribbean.

These refuelling missions, as well as *UA's* experiments, were so successful that an entirely new type of wolf pack concept was planned for May 1942, when the converted Type XB minelayer, *U116* (Korvkpt Werner von Schmidt) would be ready. The proposal was to send a self-contained wolf pack with its own independent supply submarine. *U116* sailed from Kiel on 4 April 1942, called at Heligoland and Bergen before running south to Lorient, where minor repairs were undertaken and she was provisioned. *U96* (ObLtzS Hans-Jürgen Hellriegel), the first boat of this self-contained pack named *Hecht* (Pike) was already under way, having left Brest on 23 April 1942, and another five boats followed independently on different days from St Nazaire and La Pallice, so that they would not draw

attention to the fact that a closed unit was being dispatched. These were all Type VII boats, except *U124* (Kptlt Jochen Mohr), which was an older Type IXB. This pack is of special interest because, until this point, boats travelled the shortest distance to the United States to save fuel. This time, this self-contained wolf pack was going to sweep across through the Allied convoy routes, as a fast moving formation, and, it was hoped, catch a few convoys on the way.

This plan paid dividends halfway across when *U124* overtook the just over 40 ships of convoy ONS92, on their way west from the United Kingdom. Luckily for group *Hecht*, two other U-boats were so close by that an attack could commence that coming night, while surprise was still on the German side. Once again, it is exceedingly difficult to reconstruct what actually happened because all reports contain a good number of confusing details and there appears to be no British record of some of the ships seen by U-boat lookouts to have sunk. It would appear that *U124* commenced the attack a few minutes before 02.00 hours on 12 May 1943 and observed three sinking ships, although Jürgen Rohwer could identify only two of them. The first one of these, the 7,065grt *Empire Dell*, under Cpt Hugh Mackinnon, was hardly a year old and had been chosen as a target for two reasons. First, she was among the largest in the convoy and, secondly, she was carrying a fighter

Above: The boat from which this photo was taken is probably *U461*. The oil pipe can be seen floating over to a VIIC boat, while a third U-boat is closing in to join the group.

catapult on the bows, meaning her loss would result in less interference during daylight of the next day, when contact would have to be maintained until further attacks could be launched during the following night. Of course, at the time no one in U124 was aware of the fact that there was no recovery method for the old fighters and they therefore had to be ditched after their one and only flight.

U569 (Kptlt Peter Hinsch) and U94 (ObLtzS Otto Ites) got in before U124 managed a second attack at 04.00 hours. Hinsch scored a hit after a long torpedo run of three minutes and watched a freighter sink amidst a sheet of flames, but, once again, the ship has not been identified. Ites sunk the 5,630grt Panamanian freighter Cocle and then Mohr scored hits on the 4,371grt Greek steamer Mount Parnes and the British freighter Cristales. The snag with these attacks was that the U-boats were not left in peace to fire all their torpedoes and found escorts bearing down on them at great speed. This meant that aiming was not only carried out by relatively inexperienced men but also while they were under great duress, so that there were bound to be a good number of failures. The Cristales (Cpt Hugh Roberts) was one of these. Carrying general cargo and 10 passengers, she had sailed from Milford Haven in South Wales with a high proportion of extremely heavy china clay, but despite this, did not go down as Mohr hoped. Instead there was ample time for HMCS Shediac and USCG Spencer to pick up all of the crew, gunners, airmen and passengers before sinking the badly mauled victim with gunfire.

Otto Ites, one-time watch officer of the most successful boat of World War 2 (U48), had served under three legendary commanders and now made good use of what he had learned to keep tags on the convoy and attack it twice more during the coming night, sinking the British freighter Batna and the Swedish ship Tolken. Following that he was driven off once more and the merchant ships seemed to vanish from the face of the earth. Whatever happened, none of the U-boats made further contact, leaving the convoy in peace to continue its voyage to the New World. In all, seven ships were sunk, although the wartime estimated total added up to 10 or so.

Despite this relatively heavy loss from convoy ONS92, special intelligence in Britain stated that all the attacking U-boats were driven off, and maintained that the rate of sinkings in convoys was considerably lower than among independents going it alone. This gave British authorities substantial concern because the number of ships going down in United States waters was still increasing, despite noticeable counter-attacks on U-boats. There is a rather classic report where Commander Rodger Winn (head of the secret Submarine Tracking Room in London) complained to the American authorities that they were losing rather a high number of ships in their waters and when there was no response from an admiral he said dryly, 'The trouble is that a high proportion of those ships are ours.' Despite the United States having taken some small measures to protect shipping running along the east coast, much of the southern waters were left effectively unprotected. The number of U-boats at sea had increased considerably, with the average rising to a new high of over 50. This resulted in some 125 ships being sunk during the month of May, demonstrating quite clearly that group Hecht's contribution with the first submersible supply tanker was only a tiny fraction of the total.

Although group Hecht achieved some promising success against convoy ONS92, the U-boats quickly learned that sinkings were exceedingly hard to achieve and they were more likely to see aggressive escorts bearing down on them at full speed, rather than spot slow merchant ships plodding through the torpedo sight. U406 (Kptlt Horst Dieterichs) sighted convoy ONS94, but his signal to base to call in the rest of the pack was also intercepted by HF/DF aboard escorts and it was not long before he was driven off, to be punished with several hours of depth charging. Such incidents became the order of the day, although U124 and U94 did get close enough to sink ships from convoys ONS100 and ONS102. On the whole it was diesel trouble, bad weather and the still persistent torpedo failures which prevented further progress. Many boats came home with visible damage, as well as success pennants fluttering from the extended periscope.

Organising such voyages lasting well over a month was, in itself, no mean feat and involved considerable effort from a vast network of supporters. In addition to the obvious, such as dockyard workers and the supply system, a massive mound of paperwork had to be prepared for each commander. This was now becoming more than just a time-consuming occupation, but also largely pointless because much of the information was out of date by the time men had to act on it. Therefore the U-boat Command changed the system of how individual boats were controlled. Up to this period of time, every commander was handed a specially prepared document with the latest information he was likely to require. Now, with large numbers crossing the Atlantic, some four weeks or more passed between the compilation of the details and the beginning of the operation. Therefore the individual briefings for commanders were abandoned and each boat was given a loose-leaf file to store all relevant news, including radio messages and latest intelligence from Berlin. This folder was kept up to date in the radio room and handed to flotilla staff once the boat came back into port so that land-based officers could continue maintaining it until the boat's commander returned to pick it up again. That way, at least, every boat received the latest news as soon as it became available and crews in port were unlikely to miss out on important snippets while they were away on leave.

Strangely enough, although Bletchley Park was locked out of the four-wheel Enigma code, which the cryptanalysts called 'Shark', it was still possible to work out that U-boats were being supplied at sea. But, of course, there was no easy way of finding the critical locations where this was being carried out. What was more, there was no way of telling whether there were surface or submersible vessels at work, although it was known from other intelligence that special submarine tankers were on their way. The sterling work of predicting the number and the types of submarines likely to appear was carried out in Britain by a photograph interpreter, David Brachi, who studied aerial pictures of the shipyards. By measuring the length and width of boats lying on the stocks over a period of time he could calculate how long it took before a single keel became a completed boat. This fascinating contribution to winning the battles in the Atlantic is explained in a most colourful manner by Constance Babington Smith in her fantastic book Evidence in Camera. Yet, knowing that the boats were likely to be at sea was one thing, finding them over the vastness of the ocean was another, and interference did not come until the end of 1942, when a heroic act by a few men from HMS Petard made it possible for Bletchley Park to gain an insight into the new German Enigma code.

Above: Probably *U490* (ObLtzS Wilhelm Gerlach), one of the purpose-built supply submarines. The deck was made as wide as possible so that a large number of men could work at the same time. The 37mm quick-firing deck gun was somewhat useless and was hardly ever used.

Above: 'The Wild Moritz' himself. Korvkpt Georg von Wilamowitz-Moellendorf (in light-coloured uniform) served in U-boats during World War 1 and was one of the oldest U-boat commanders.

Left: U459 (Korvkpt Georg von Wilamowitz-Moellendorf), showing the sweeping lines of the massive, snow-covered upper deck.

Right: Three boats meeting on the high seas. One problem with the standard naval inflatables was that they were designed as emergency lifeboats for holding men and the bottoms were not strong enough for carrying heavy packages, especially if these had sharp edges.

Below: U407 meeting *U96* during September 1942, showing how difficult it was to work on the upper deck in all but the calmest of conditions.

Above: U530 (Kptlt Kurt Lange) meeting *U172* (Kptlt Carl Emmermann).

Above: Otto Ites (third from left), commander of *U146* and *U94* and Knight of the Iron Cross, seen here as watch officer of *U48*.

Chapter 13

Far–Off Waters March–August 1942

It is important to bear in mind that the initial attacks against the United States accounted for only a small fraction of the total U-boat force. There were also a good number of boats off Norway, in the Arctic, and in the Mediterranean, while in addition a major thrust was also planned to hit oil installations in the Caribbean. This became quite a headache in that it was the first time that a large number of boats were dispatched into tropical waters and specialised equipment was called for on an unprecedented scale. The snag was that German colonial activities had been curtailed at the end of World War 1 and naval experiences in hot climates were somewhat out of date. A few individual boats had gone south — enduring interior temperatures like those of a moderate baking oven — and so the U-boat Command could call on a number of experienced officers for advice. However, there was very little which could be done to help the crews, because their boats lacked the basic requirements for such a hostile climate. The idyllic islands of the Caribbean tend to conjure up visions of paradise in crystal clear water. Yet, for men in submarines, this was going to be nothing short of hell on earth. Boats were not only without air conditioning but they also lacked even a basic ventilation system, meaning the interior would get hot, damp or even wet and the men were likely to suffer a variety of tropically induced

discomforts in addition to lookouts' sunburn. Even the endless supply of coffee, which had sustained so many in the cold Atlantic, would not lift morale under such conditions and large stocks of beer and lemonade were be taken along. Lemonade could be carried in concentrated form and diluted when required; whether boats carried a high proportion of beer depended on where the crew came from. Bavarians were unlikely to do anything unless they were well irrigated — and in those days it was customary for civilian employers to supply labourers with several litres per day. Therefore boats with a high proportion of men from the deep south were provided with an above average supply of beer.

The plan was to attack Aruba, Curaçao, the Paranagua peninsula, Guiana and Trinidad with the first wave. U-boats were told to go in and use torpedoes against ships in the harbours and then, if conditions permitted, to attack a second time to shell oil, power and harbour installations on land. Co-ordinating such a project from an operations room in France was going to be more than difficult, especially as almost all

Below: Aerial depth charges splashing into the water. As with their ship-launched equivalents, they were fitted with pressure-sensitive detonators and could be adjusted to explode at any depth.

Left: This depth charge thrower was photographed aboard a German warship, but gives some idea of what the main weapon against submarines looked like. Some of these drums were dropped off a rack at the stern of the ship, while others were thrown a good distance by an explosive charge in their rod-like base.

valuable intelligence came from the prewar period, with only a few snippets added later from neutral sources. The plan was for the West Indies group, under the cover name of *Neuland*, to send a short signal from 40° West, risking being caught by radio direction finders, but essential if the U-boat Command was to know whether the boats had crossed the danger zone of the Atlantic. Following this, a simultaneous attack was planned to commence shortly before dawn on 16 February 1942. The results were quite interesting, with apparently stronger opposition than was experienced by the first boats of Operation *Paukenschlag*. However, by making use of a new moon period, the majority of U-boats were able to expend their torpedoes in a relatively short time. This resulted in harbours being shut down, which denied the U-boats further targets. Yet, despite such widespread defensive measures, the authorities were good enough to announce the details over the radio in plain language.

Group *Neuland* was supported by a second wave, consisting of the incredibly powerful force of *U126* (Kptlt Ernst Bauer) going it alone. The 'snag' was that targets were still so plentiful that, despite arriving two weeks after the first wave, *U126* had expended all torpedoes in two weeks, sinking nine ships, and had to return with group *Neuland*, thus leaving the enemy unaware that two waves had attacked. The boats were already chugging back home when Dönitz was surprised by a terse memorandum from Admiral Raeder, saying the Caribbean should not be left empty of U-boats and pointing out the importance of keeping enemy forces tied up in those waters. Once again, Dönitz delicately pointed out that he could not occupy an operations area if he did not have the necessary boats. The problem was rectified a few weeks later by dispatching another wave together with a supply submarine.

At the time when the boats were making their first inroads in the Caribbean, there was the other pressing problem of sending boats to reconnoitre the area off Freetown, Africa. The reason was that much of the traffic running up and down the Atlantic had been passing through the Pan-American Neutrality Zone, which was declared shortly after the outbreak of the war with the terse message that the security of that area would be maintained by the United States. Now, when America's entry into the war had resulted in the dissolution of that area, it was thought that British merchant shipping which had been taking advantage of it would be likely to return to its old prewar routes through the eastern Atlantic. *U68* (Korvkpt Karl-Friedrich Merten) and *U505* (Korvkpt Axel-Olaf Loewe, the boat which was later captured by the United States) were the first to be sent into this area. Although both boats found less merchant shipping than had formerly used this route, they did run into enough independents for *U68* to sink seven and *U505* four ships towards the end of February and in early March 1942.

All these operations in far-off waters ran relatively smoothly, with some minor exceptions. There was the case reported by Jochen Brennecke in *Hunters and the Hunted* where one U-boat went to action stations for a torpedo attack when smoke was sighted, only to find it was a bonfire on a small island. And it has already been mentioned that *U156* (Korvkpt Werner Hartenstein), the boat more famous for the sinking of the liner *Laconia*, tried using its deck gun without first removing the tampion, seriously injuring two men who were later landed on Martinique for hospital treatment. However, the majority of these problems were put down to a lack of experience rather than gross negligence.

The really pressing difficulty did not occur in the far-off regions but nearer home, where several worrying trends developed, with three boats vanishing in mysterious circumstances. First, *U82* (Kptlt Siegfried Rollmann) disappeared around 2 February 1942, then *U587* (Kptlt Ulrich Borcherdt) on 26 March and *U252* (Kptlt Kai Lerchen) on 15 April. Lerchen, incidentally, had his birth registered in the east end of London, but that had nothing to do with the mystery. His parents were on their way home from South Africa to Germany and it was a legal requirement to register births at sea in the next port of call. The strange combination which made the U-boat Command highly suspicious was that all three were crossing the Bay of Biscay on their way home when they reported a poorly protected convoy, shortly before vanishing from the ether. Thinking that there were hunter-killer groups at large, similar to the Q-ships of World War 1, Dönitz forbade attacks against convoys in this critical area of 10°–15° West and 42°–50° North, and told commanders to keep their eyes open for anything suspicious. As it happened, all three boats chanced to stumble upon ordinary convoys, OS18, WS17 and OG82, which for some reason were not tracked by the B-Dienst and therefore did not appear in the usual intelligence reports passed to the U-boat Command.

Changes were afoot, making the Atlantic an ever-increasingly dangerous battleground. The most significant of these was the introduction of the so-called Hedgehog, an ahead-throwing anti-submarine mortar, holding six rows of four shells — 24 in all. Depth charges, used so far against submarines, had several disadvantages, the biggest being that asdic contact was lost once the attacking ship got close to the target submarine. Therefore, the hunter had to drop depth charges blind and hope that they were tossed on to the correct spot. This problem was overcome by organising escorts to operate as a team so that one would maintain asdic contact while it directed another to drop the depth charges, but even this presented a problem because the disturbance caused by the detonation lasted long enough for the U-boat to attempt a getaway and the whole hunting process had to start anew. The other snag was that the ship had to move at considerable speed when dropping depth charges. Otherwise it risked having its stern blown off. In fact there were several occasions when hunters were badly mauled by their own depth charges. The Hedgehog had the advantage that its charges were not only thrown a good distance ahead but they only exploded on contact. Therefore, there was no disturbance with a miss. And the other significant point was that it did not allow the U-boat commander time to move out of the way while the ship passed overhead. About 60 escort ships were fitted with Hedgehogs by the early summer of 1942.

This is not to say that depth charges were becoming obsolete. In fact they had gone through considerable development and modification since the beginning of the war. So much so, that some officers treated the newer types with considerable mistrust. The new twin-screw class corvettes were being fitted with new, quick loading depth charges, capable of being fired from the bridge, rather than by someone standing by the side of each thrower. What was more, the control for this could be adjusted to dispatch quite complicated patterns and discharge these automatically with the correct time delay.

Below: A depth charge exploding.

Chapter 14
The First Double Wolf Pack
July–December 1942

The fascinating developments during the second half of 1942 have largely been concealed by overzealous historians producing a somewhat distorted image of what actually happened. The general picture tends to be one of doom for Britain, with U-boats coming close to winning the Battle of the Atlantic. Yet, although there is some statistical basis for such an assumption, it is also most misleading and one wonders whether this impression was spread on purpose to help curtail a wave of unrest in the country or to spur the working classes into making even greater sacrifices. Whatever, the total sinking figures achieved by U-boats may have reached an all-time high, but it must be remembered that this was due to there having been a vast number of them at sea. The important, and often forgotten, point is that the majority never even saw the enemy and the performance of each individual boat dropped most dramatically into another frustrating low. During the first 'Happy Time' in 1940, each boat at sea was sinking over five ships per month. Early in 1942, during the so-called 'Second Happy Time' in American waters, these figures rose again, but only reached an average of two ships sunk per month per U-boat at sea. For the autumn of that year the results fell even further, down to one merchant ship being sunk per month per U-boat at sea. What is more, this figure of one merchant ship sunk per U-boat was not reached during October and December. A maximum of about 100 ships were being sunk by about 100 U-boats at sea, but this force carried well over 1,000 torpedoes, so the potential hitting power was enormous when compared with the totals actually achieved.

Historians want us to believe that the climax of the Battle of the Atlantic occurred during March 1943, when the fast convoy HX229 caught up with the slow convoy SC122 just as a massive wolf pack was about to strike. This may have resulted in the largest convoy battle of all time, but it quickly loses its significance when one considers that the magic number of 100 U-boats at sea had been reached the previous September. In other words, such a massive concentration remained at sea for a period of over half a year before a clash of titans took place. So, in many ways, the most significant point to note between August 1942 and March 1943 was that Germany had potential wolf packs at sea for massive convoy battles, but that no large-scale attacks ever took place.

The intriguing conundrum with those few actions which did take place is that they occurred at a time when Britain had, once more, gained an insight into the German radio code whereas wolf packs were avoided very well during the so-called intelligence blackout. One of the new, four-wheel Enigma machines, as well as the necessary books to understand its code, was captured by men from HMS *Petard* on 30 October 1942, when Lieutenant Anthony Fasson, Sub-Lieutenant Gordon Connel, Able Seaman Colin Grazier and Canteen Assistant Tommy Brown managed to get on board *U559* (Kptlt Hans Heidtmann) before it went down in the eastern Mediterranean. Fasson and Grazier were still inside the U-boat when it sank, but in an incredibly short time they had handed up enough secret material for Bletchley Park to regain the key to the Atlantic code, which they called 'Shark'.

Before looking at the actions of late 1942, to establish why a massive convoy battle did not take place earlier, it might be appropriate to examine the options open to the U-boat Command when the 'Second Happy Time' in American waters was drawing to a close. Forecasting this decline was not difficult. Sinking figures reached a peak early in the year, during the so-called 'Second Happy Time' in American waters, but then degenerated steadily for the rest of the year. Following the unhindered success of the first couple of months, every returning U-boat reported an increase in retaliatory measures. The 'Second Happy Time' was still in full swing when *U68* and *U505* were sent south on exploratory missions to confirm the suspicion that the dissolution of the Pan-American Neutrality Zone had resulted in shipping returning to the old, prewar routes along the eastern Atlantic. Their reconnaissance suggested that it would be profitable to send long-range U-boats south of Gibraltar, to concentrate on traffic running along the African coast. At the same time another wolf pack might find good targets by concentrating on refrigerated transports bringing meat from the Argentine. Consequently, the Freetown to Cape Town route and the Amazon and La Plata estuaries were suggested as new operational areas.

The North Atlantic presented far greater problems because severe retaliation and strong anti-submarine forces had to be taken into account. Land-based aircraft, flying up to about 500 miles out to sea, were more than a mere nuisance. They prevented U-boats from shadowing convoys and thus frustrated the entire wolf pack concept. Not long before, Admiral Dönitz had claimed that aircraft could not harm submarines, saying that it was similar to crows not being able to hurt moles. However, by the end of 1942, this confidence was shattered to such an extent that he was forced to change this opinion and ask for conning towers to be modified so that they could carry effective anti-aircraft guns. At that stage it was estimated that it would be the middle of the following year before sufficient U-boats with stronger guns could challenge aircraft at sea.

With Allied land-based aircraft flying so far out to sea, the unprotected air gap in mid-Atlantic had been reduced to a narrow zone of about 300 miles which meant the Germans had no alternative other than to choose this strip as their main operating zone. The prospects of going south, into the waters between Britain and Gibraltar, did not appeal because that was where the heavy losses of December 1941 had occurred. The main problem with those southerly routes was that their entire length could be patrolled by aircraft, making U-boat operations exceedingly hazardous.

The debate about new operational areas was taking place against a backdrop of internal turmoil within the High Command. The authorities in Berlin agreed that Dönitz's headquarters in a bunker attached to an old villa in Kernével near Lorient might be well protected from bombs, but they pointed out that being so close to the coast placed it in an all too vulnerable location in the event of a raid by land troops. Dönitz didn't agree. His maxim had always been to lead from the front and he had now risen high enough up the pecking order not to let himself be intimidated by stuffy, desk-bound admirals. However, during March 1942, his resistance was suddenly shattered by the daring British commando attack on St Nazaire, which made it quite plain that a safer location was going to be essential. Yet, finding a suitable alternative was not easy and most of the suggested locations were rejected for one reason or another. Finally, Dönitz agreed to move to Avenue Maréchal Maunoury in Paris, where the headquarters of the U-boat Command remained until March 1943. Plans formulated around the time of the move centred on the assumption that wolf pack operations would resume in the North Atlantic during the autumn, when long dark nights and the seasonal bad weather provided ideal conditions. These ideas had hardly been developed when the Organisation Department in Germany, under Hans-Georg von Friedeburg, announced that an unexpectedly high number of U-boats would be appearing at the front as early as June or July. The reason was that they had been frozen in their Baltic bases by solid ice during the exceptionally harsh weather of the preceding winter, meaning training schedules had to be curtailed. Yet, the building yards continued to keep their production lines running to result in a most welcome bulge appearing at the front. In view of this it was early summer rather than autumn when the first wolf pack was poised to resume the all-important convoy war in the mid-Atlantic air gap.

This new offensive got off to a promising start, when group *Hai* was sent south to intercept convoy OS33 by forming a patrol line near the Azores. Of course, at the time, no one in Germany had any idea about the identity of the convoy and the position of the line had to be adjusted according to radio intercepts from the B-Dienst. At first considerable confusion was created by the convoy splitting in two, but the few U-boats in contact noticed that one group continued heading south along the eastern side of the Atlantic while the other section turned off towards South America. Strangely enough it was the pack's supply boat, rather than the main force, which continued shadowing to make the first strike at 00.22 hours on 12 July 1942. Luckily for the Germans *U116* (Korvkpt Werner von Schmidt) was a large Type XB minelayer with two stern torpedo tubes, which made it possible to attack the 7,093grt British freighter *Cortona*. A purpose-built Type XIV supply boat could not, of course, have launched such an assault because these did not carry any torpedo tubes at all. The 'eels' were still running when *U201* (Kptlt Adalbert Schnee) aimed at the same target. Yet, despite at least two hits within three minutes, none of them caused the ship to sink and *U201* later shot another torpedo into the stationary wreck to give the *coup de grâce*. This, together with other similar incidents, provided the sickening evidence that there still had to be a major fault with the torpedoes.

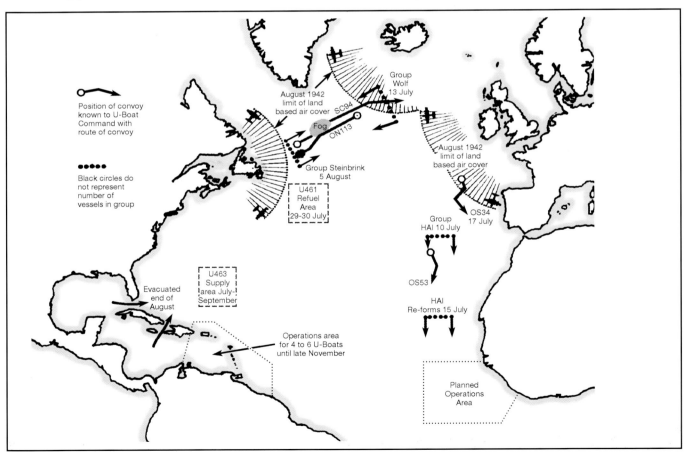

Above: U-boat operations, July–August 1942. Group *Steinbrink*, which attacked Convoy SC94, was made up of the following U-boats: *U71* (ObltzS Hardo Rodler von Roithberg), *U210*, (Kptlt Rudolf Lamcke), *U379* (Kptlt Paul-Hugo Kettner), *U454* (Kptlt Burkhard Hackländer), *U461* (Korvkpt Wolf Stiebler), *U463* (Korvkpt Leo Wolfbauer), *U593* (Kptlt Gerd Kelbling), *U597* (Kptlt Eberhard Bopst), *U607* (Kptlt Ernst Mengersen) and *U704* (Kptlt Horst Kessler).
Group *Wolf* was made up of the following U-boats: *U43*, (ObltzS Hans-Joachim Schwantke), *U71*, (ObltzS Hardo Rodler von Roithberg), *U86* (Kptlt Walter Schug), *U90*, (Kptlt Hans-Jürgen Oldörp), *U379* (Kptlt Paul-Hugo Kettner), *U454* (Kptlt Burkhard Hackländer), *U552* (Korvkpt Erich Topp), *U597* (Kptlt Eberhard Bopst), *U607* (Kptlt Ernst Mengersen) and *U704* (Kptlt Horst Kessler).

Soon after this, *U582* (Kptlt Werner Schulte) entered the inferno to help sink a total of six ships. Two other boats from the pack, probably sent especially to confuse historians by having almost identical numbers, *U572* (Kptlt Heinz Hirsacker) and *U752* (Korvkpt Karl-Ernst Schroeter) did not manage to get into a shooting position. Neither did *U136* (Kptlt Heinrich Zimmermann), which had already been sunk with all hands by the escorts *Pelican*, *Spey* and *Leopard*, a few days before *U116* made contact. The initial success against convoy OS33 quickly degenerated into more confusion and a pronounced inability to penetrate the escort screen during the following night. Consequently the remaining ships reached their destination unmolested, while a number of peeved U-boat men nursed wounds and some minor damage.

Just over a fortnight later, Kptlt Hans-Heinz Linder (*U202*) accidentally ran into convoy OS34 while on his way back from American waters and succeeded in shadowing it long enough for two other boats, also on their way home from the western Atlantic, to approach for an attack. Together, *U564* (Kptlt Reinhard Suhren), *U108* (Korvkpt Klaus Scholtz) and *U202* succeeded in sinking two ships, although the wartime estimated total was four sunk and a further five damaged. The interesting point about this was that all three boats were returning with a plentiful supply of torpedoes from the once lucrative western Atlantic. Until a short time earlier on this station U-boats' ammunition usually ran out long before food and fuel. Another point, even more telling, but missed both by the men aboard the U-boats and by the U-boat Command, was that the shadowing process was made especially difficult by the presence of a large, land-based aircraft, although the action was taking place well beyond what had previously been believed to be the maximum range of 500 miles from the nearest base. This indicated that the Allies were pulling out every stop to penetrate further and further into the air gap, assuring that it would not be long before it closed completely.

At about the same time as the battle for convoy OS34 raged in southern waters, the first wolf pack for several months was assembled some 600 miles west of Ireland, with the aim of sweeping towards Newfoundland and then turning south along the American coast until it reached the Caribbean. However, group *Wolf* never got that far. On 13 July 1942, *U71* (Kptlt Hardo Rodler von Treuberg), on the northern extremity of the patrol line, sighted convoy ON111. This was von Treuberg's first cruise with *U71*, but he had commanded *U24* for nine months and before that served as watch officer in *U96* under Kptlt Heinrich Lehmann-Willenbrock for almost a year. In addition to this, the majority of his crew had participated in several operational cruises, meaning that none of them were inexperienced newcomers, but somehow they succeeded in

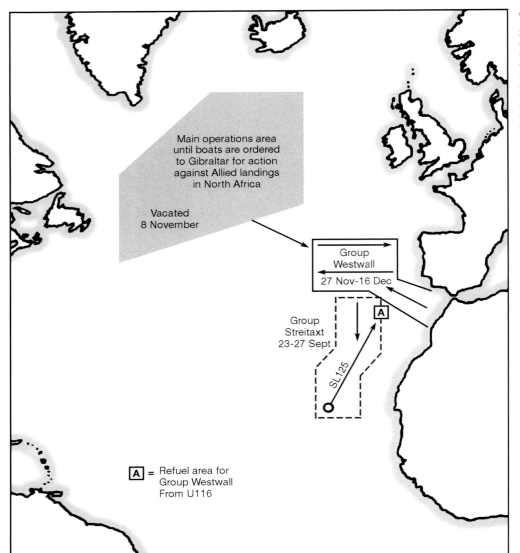

Main operations area until boats are ordered to Gibraltar for action against Allied landings in North Africa

Vacated 8 November

Group Westwall
27 Nov-16 Dec

Group Streitaxt 23-27 Sept

SL 125

A

A = Refuel area for Group Westwall From U116

generating considerable confusion by sending garbled messages, causing the U-boat Command to direct group *Wolf* northwards to intercept an eastbound convoy. By the time it was realised that the target was heading west, it was already too late. The merchant ships were beyond reach. After this, poor visibility and exceedingly rough weather frustrated further attacks, despite the B-Dienst providing a number of good, clear intercepts about convoy routes in that area. The few U-boats making contact with merchant ships found themselves driven off by exceptionally frisky escorts, leaving group *Wolf* with little alternative other than to head towards *U461* (Korvkpt Wolf-Harro Stiebler), one of the purpose-built Type XIV supply boats, on its first operational cruise. Following this, the refreshed boats from group *Wolf* set about finding more traffic in the area between Newfoundland and Britain.

The convoy war trudged on in this vein. Several groups of merchant ships were intercepted, but each time only a few U-boats succeeded in approaching close enough to shoot. There was always a gremlin or two somewhere along the line to prevent a notable success. The *Lohs* patrol line of a dozen or so boats, for example, was ordered west so that it could commence a search for convoy SC95 as soon as it became light on 13 August 1942.

Once again the position of the 27 ships was provided by intercepts from the B-Dienst. KptIt Odo Loewe (*U256*) even sighted them on the 15th and continued shadowing until darkness, when he was driven off. Only one of the two boats he managed to call in came close enough to launch torpedoes, but KptIt Karl-Horst Horn's (*U705*) effort resulted in the sinking of only one small ship, the American 3,279grt freighter *Balladier*. Neither *U256* nor *U605* (KptIt Herbert-Victor Schütze) managed to launch torpedoes and both had to withdraw empty handed. So, in all, although a dozen U-boats were milling about in mid-Atlantic, the majority were doing very little other than disturbing the sleep patterns of the men aboard the escorts.

Loewe, incidentally, had commissioned *U256* shortly before Christmas of 1941, some eight months earlier, and this was his first operational war cruise. Schütze and Horn, had similar backgrounds. Both of them had been at sea as commanders of new boats for about two weeks of their first operational war cruise, with inexperienced crews when this action took place, and it is quite likely that seasickness was a significant problem aboard all boats.

Following the attack against convoy SC95, 10 boats from group *Lohs* sailed to a secret refuelling location some 500 miles

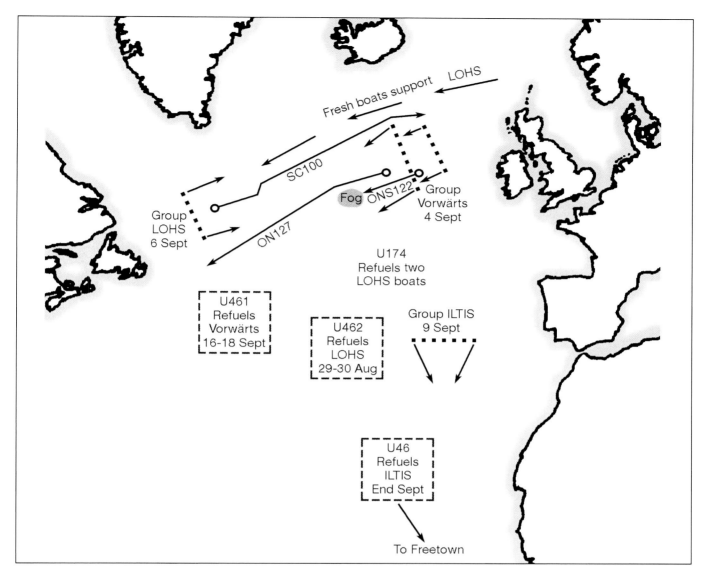

Above: U-boat operations August–September 1942. Group *Lohs*, which attacked Convoys SC95, SC97 and ON129, comprised:
U135 (Kptlt Friedrich-Hermann Praetorius), *U174* (Fregkpt Ulrich Thilo), *U176* (Korvkpt Reiner Dierksen), *U256* (Kptlt Odo Loewe), *U373* (Kptlt Paul-Karl Loeser), *U432* (Kptlt Heinz-Otto Schultze), *U438* (Kptlt Rudolf Franzius), *U461* (Korvkpt Wolf Stiebler), *U462* (ObltzS Bruno Vowe), *U569* (Kptlt Gunter Jahn), *U605* (Kptlt Herbert Viktor Schütze), *U660* (Kptlt Götz Bauer), *U705* (Kptlt Karl-Horst Horn) and *U755* (Kptlt Walter Göing).
Group *Vorwärts* comprised *U91* (Kptlt Heinz Walkerling), *U92* (Kptlt Adolf Oelrich), *U211* (Kptlt Karl Hause), *U407* (Kptlt Ernst-Ulrich Brüller), *U409* (ObltzS Hans-Ferdinand Massmann), *U411* (ObltzS Gerhard Litterscheid), *U604* (Kptlt Horst Höltring), *U609* (Kptlt Klaus Rudloff), *U659* (Kptlt Hans Stock) and *U756* (Kptlt Klaus Harney).

west of the Azores, where they met *U462* (ObLtzS Bruno Vowe), which was still on its first war cruise, having left Kiel on 23 July 1942. So far, group *Loh*s had been searching through the shipping lanes between the North Channel (the stretch of water between Ireland and Scotland) and Newfoundland in Canada, while other boats were operating further south, between Gibraltar and Freetown (Sierra Leone in Africa), but this group was so small that it could hardly be called a co-ordinated wolf pack. While group *Lohs* was refuelling, there were enough boats heading west to establish two packs in the vital communication lines between Britain and North America. The majority of the *Lohs* boats were still with *U462* when the first new boats formed into group *Stier*, but this patrol line was quickly amalgamated with group *Vorwärts* to form one long string of submarines, stretching out like a passive drift net, hoping the quarry would arrive to become entangled in it. This happened quite quickly,

despite indications that Britain knew the German positions and therefore routed convoy SC97 northwards, around the top of the newly extended patrol line. It can't have been an accident that the merchant ships bumped into the line's northern extremities, rather than being caught firmly in its middle. *U609* (ObLtzS Klaus Rudolff) responded quickly by launching an underwater attack shortly after 10.00 hours on 31 August 1942, sinking the 5,625grt Panamanian freighter *Capria* and the 4,663grt Norwegian *Bronxville*, but the rest of the pack was too far away to make an impression on SC97.

Although the patrol line was exceedingly long, the next convoy (ON127) also tried to avoid it, this time by sailing around its southern flank on 9 September. The merchant ships had almost escaped, by losing their shadow during darkness of the coming night, but contact was regained the next day and shortly afterwards *U96* (ObLtzS Hans-Jürgen Hellriegel) shot three torpedoes in three minutes, commencing at 16.30 hours on the 10th. Once again, there were indications of torpedoes not functioning properly. The 12,190grt British tanker *F. J. Wolfe*, was hit, but managed to reach port. Yet, this attack did send two other ships (the 4,241grt Belgian freighter *Elisabeth van Belgie* and the 6,313grt Norwegian tanker *Sveve*) to the bottom. Although *U96* was driven off before all torpedoes could be fired, sufficient contact was maintained for Kptlt Hans Stock (*U659*) to attack four hours later. Once again things did not go too well. He hit an 8,029grt tanker, *Empire Oil*, with two torpedoes, but failed to sink her. *U584* (Kptlt Joachim Deecke) later had to expend a third torpedo for the *coup de grâce*. In addition to this, *U404* (Kptlt Otto von Bülow), *U608* (ObLtzS Rolf Struckmeier), *U218* (Kptlt Richard Becker), *U92* (ObLtzS Adolf Oelrich), *U380* Kptlt Josef Röther) and *U211* (Kptlt Karl Hause, who had been promoted only during the previous week) all came within shooting range to sink a reported 19 ships. However, the confusion was such that the U-boat Command could not determine the exact location of the attacks nor the correct totals. After the war this figure was modified to seven ships sunk and four damaged. The escort *Ottawa* was also sunk by *U92*, but warships tended to be excluded in the running totals. Despite close analysis, it is quite likely that these figures require further modification once log books are studied in detail, but bearing in mind that the majority of wolf packs were frustrated by eager escorts, this was indeed a major victory for U-boats.

While group *Vorwärts* was chasing convoy ON127 westwards, the remaining boats of group *Lohs* returned to the Newfoundland Banks, where *U216* (Kptlt Karl-Otto Schulz) sighted convoy SC99 on the 13th, just two weeks after having left Kiel for its first operational voyage. This unusual Type VIID minelayer had the same torpedo armament as a standard VIIC, but on this occasion the escorts were too quick, forcing it under before any could be fired. As a result, the convoy was lost until it was rediscovered by *U440* (Kptlt Hans Geissler) during the following day. This inexperienced boat, which had left Kiel three days after *U216*, suffered even worse. Caught in the middle of a depth charge attack, the men were lucky to survive. They resurfaced once the coast was clear, but then required help from other boats before they could attempt the return voyage to Brest. Boats still in formation were joined by more newcomers from Germany to be given the name *Pfeil*, but this fresh approach did not produce any more successes. Once again a convoy, this time ON129, was sighted at the extreme end of the patrol line, making it virtually impossible for the rest of the pack to reach it. Following this, natural protection, in the form of persistent fog instead of zealous escorts, forced the U-boat Command to break the action off. It was argued that the appalling visibility would soon be replaced by land-based aircraft and therefore it would be better to move further away from the Canadian coast. When this happened, the patrol line was dissolved and each boat operated on its own until ordered into a new formation, though by this time the majority of commanders at sea were newcomers, who were kept on exceedingly short apron strings and given constant advice about what they should do.

Above: U219 (Type XB minelayer) on the right. The 12 mineshafts along the starboard side are clearly visible as black circles. The first of these boats was ready to go to sea at a time when there were still problems with the special shaft mines and many of these boats were employed for supply duties or as transports, rather than the laying of mines.

Chapter 15

Successful Failures October 1942–January 1943

Finding convoys, shadowing them and then approaching to within torpedo launching range had become the most significant problem for wolf packs. The earlier technique of sailing with the convoy, selecting the biggest targets from point-blank range, aiming carefully and then picking them off at leisure was no longer possible. There were literally no more than a handful of occasions when a boat remained within shooting range for any length of time. One of those rare occasions occurred shortly before 06.00 hours on 13 October 1942, when Kptlt Hans-Hartwig Trojer of *U221* fired his first shot against convoy SC104, sinking the 2,342grt Norwegian freighter *Fangerstern*. For 25 minutes he dodged about until it was possible to get an unobstructed aim at the 5,227grt British freighter *Ashworth*. Even this commotion did not bring immediate retribution, making it possible for him also to sink the 3,785grt Norwegian freighter *Senta* a few minutes later. Despite this carnage, *U221* stayed with the convoy for another half hour before emptying its remaining tubes, but nothing appears to have been hit. Then the need to reload and the coming of daylight, rather than the escorts, forced Trojer to withdraw. He maintained contact throughout the day, to launch another attack shortly after midnight, when the following day was four minutes old. Once again, he remained within shooting distance for the best part of an hour. The last vessel from convoy SC104 to sink was a tiny landing craft being carried on the deck of the whale factory ship *Southern Empress*. *U221's* shadowing effort also paid dividends inasmuch that *U607* (Kptlt Ernst Mengersen), *U661* (ObLtzS Erich von Lilienfeld) and *U618* (ObLtzS Kurt Baberg) approached close enough to launch torpedoes and sink one ship each, but this was hardly the type of success required to force the Allies to their knees. To make matters worse, *U661* was sunk with all hands when it was rammed by the Royal Navy destroyer HMS *Viscount*, doing 25 knots.

Above: The mansion at Bletchley Park at around the time when the British government first took it over to use as a decoding centre.

All these commanders were examples of the second generation of men who had served as watch officers at the beginning of the war, when they learned their trade under difficult combat conditions. Yet, despite this experience, there was little they could do to bring their antiquated weapons to action. Although they succeeded in finding targets, convoys often passed the wolf packs at the extreme end of the patrol line, making it difficult for the majority of boats to get within striking range. This was by no means the only dilemma and the U-boat Command's war diary is littered with records of a long chain of disasters. Reading through Günter Hessler's account of the Battle of the Atlantic one will find numerous critical headings for the end of 1942, such as 'Further Decline in Caribbean Operations', 'The Last Important Concentration in the Caribbean', 'Increased Efficiency of Surface A/S Methods', 'German Radar Unsatisfactory', 'Ineffectiveness off Freetown', 'Failure off the Mouth of the Congo', 'Failure of German Intelligence' and so on. All this provides evidence that Britain kept ahead of the battles by avoiding the majority of U-boats at sea. Although unable to understand the German code until the end of November 1942, the Royal Navy's Operational Intelligence Centre, and its a highly secret Submarine Tracking Room deep inside a bunker behind Admiralty Arch in London, was able to deduce enough about U-boat movements from other intelligence to keep abreast of the Atlantic battle. The story of how Rodger Winn and a band of dedicated volunteers kept tags on U-boat movements is best described by Patrick Beesly in his fascinating book *Very Special Intelligence*.

Britain devoted considerable resources to fighting the intelligence war on a variety of fronts, while the opposite happened in Germany, where most of the efforts were channelled into muscles rather than brains. For example, finding the opposition often a step ahead resulted in one spy hunt being followed by another. Each time the higher leaders whittled down the number of people who were in the know about U-boat movements, until finally Dönitz was happy to work with an exceedingly small staff. The interesting point about these spy hunts is that they were hardly taken seriously by the Supreme Naval Command, which continued sending sensitive information to people who did not need it for their usual duties.

The struggle against technical deficiencies had started to make a significant impact by the time the United States joined the war at the beginning of 1942 and by the end of that year numerous steps had been taken to make the dilapidated U-boats more effective. New sights, so that torpedoes could be fired without having to point the whole boat at the target, had already been introduced, but special anti-convoy and anti-escort torpedoes were still on the production lines. The first mentioned was designed to run in loops, once it had reached a pre-adjusted distance in a straight line. The idea was that it then still had a chance of hitting a ship in a convoy even if it missed the target which it was being aimed at. The other torpedo, acoustically guided for coping with small escorts approaching head-on at high speed, took longer to develop and it was the autumn of 1943 before it saw its first operational service.

By the end of 1942 it was obvious that it would not be long before the air gap in the mid-Atlantic closed completely and that U-boats would have to remain submerged for longer periods. At the same time, it was necessary to have a totally new U-boat with much higher underwater speeds. Today it is well known that these electro-boats came into service just before the end of the war but early in 1943 it was thought that the first ones might be ready by mid-1944. Until then, stopgap measures had to be found if Germany was going to maintain any type of meagre grip on the battles at sea. So two important steps were taken. The first was to equip boats with stronger anti-aircraft guns and the second was to provide them with a *Schnorchel* or breathing pipe, so that they could run their diesel engines without having to surface. Incidentally, the question of how they were going to find convoys without positioning lookouts on the top of the conning tower was not as difficult as is often made out. Water is an excellent conductor of sound and it was often possible to hear ships which were too far away to be seen by lookouts. This sound detection gear did not work terribly well when boats were surfaced or using the *Schnorchel* because the noise from diesel engines and water lapping against the hull muffled its reception, but it was often used during bad visibility. Boats dived briefly so that the hydrophone operator could listen for any mechanical noises.

The other great bugbear of the time, the question of how Britain managed to detect U-boats, was answered with the idea that there were so many anti-submarine forces at work that U-boats were bound to run into them sooner or later. The fact that Britain was employing its slender resources in the most profitable areas did not occur to experts in Germany. Instead they turned their attention to radar and developed devices for detecting Allied transmissions and others for decoying both radar and asdic impulses. By the end of 1942 things had become so bad that Dönitz could see that the entire U-boat fleet was obsolete and that a totally new weapon was required. However, despite suffering severe losses, U-boats were still holding their own and it was not until May 1943 that such an unacceptably large number were sunk for him to order what he hoped would be a temporary withdrawal from the main operational area in the North Atlantic.

Below: The mansion at Bletchley Park photographed during the summer of 2000, showing a more modern extension on the building.

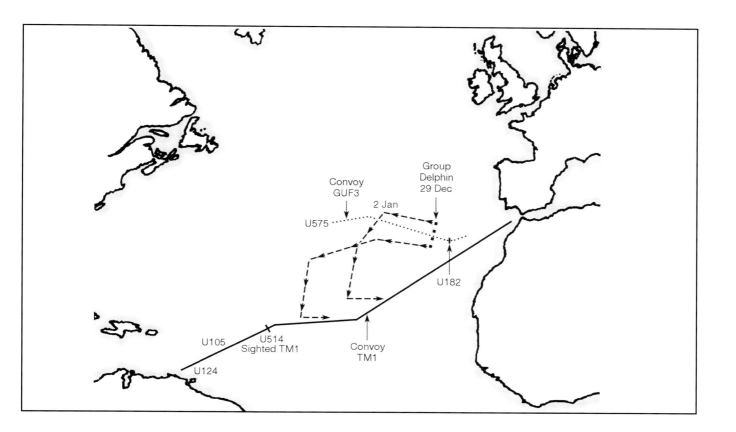

The most significant point about the last months of 1942 and the beginning of 1943 is a large number of about 100 U-boats were at sea every day without a large-scale convoy battle taking place. Again and again, the Allies avoided wolf pack after wolf pack. A few boats succeeded in finding convoys and attacked with vigour, but these were definitely lone efforts and for most of the time it was impossible to bring in the support of a wolf pack to decimate the merchant ships. In view of this, the few convoys which did see a high proportion of their ships sunk are of special interest. The tanker convoy TM1 and HX229 and SC122 spring to mind. But first, before examining these in more detail, it is necessary to look at the major change being experienced by attacking U-boats. By the end of 1942, it was virtually impossible to shadow convoys and repeat the performance of *U221*, which was mentioned at the beginning of this chapter. This major component of the wolf pack tactic was no longer paying dividends, throwing the entire concept into disarray. Two years earlier it was possible for several U-boats to expend all their torpedoes against the same convoy by chasing, attacking, reloading and then repeating the process. Now, towards the end of 1942, U-boats were lucky if they got close to a convoy on one occasion. The chances of multiple strikes were certainly exceedingly slim and U-boats could hope to sink more than one target only if they could get a salvo of torpedoes off within a matter of minutes before escorts frustrated the aiming process. A few of the luckier U-boats had opportunities to attack two or even three convoys, but their days of picking out multiple targets at leisure were over. The majority of U-boats were turned away long before they came within sight of merchant ships. On top of this, there were many more boats

Above: Convoy TM1, December 1942–January 1943. Group *Delphin* comprised *U125* (Kptlt Ulrich Folkers), *U381* (Kptlt Wilhelm Heinrich, Graf von Pückler und Limpurg), *U436* (Kptlt Günther Seibicke), *U442* (Kptlt Hans-Jürgen Hesse), *U514* (Kptlt Hans-Jürgen Affermann), *U571* (Kptlt Helmuth Möhlmann), *U575* (Kptlt Günther Heydemann) and *U620* (Kptlt Heinz Stein). Two outward-bound boats (*U511* Kptlt Fritz Schneewind and *U522* Kptlt Herbert Schneider) and two inward-bound boats (*U181* Korvkpt Wolfgang Lüth and *U134* Kptlt Rudolf Schendel) were also directed towards the convoy.

which did not even get close enough to be forced under by the outer ring of convoy escorts.

Convoy TM1 was one of the few German successes during this lean time when wolf packs were failing miserably to locate convoys. The loss of virtually a whole group of tankers destined to supply the Allied armies in northwest Africa, a short time after they had landed there, was indeed a severe blow. Although this loss can be traced back to hiccups in the Submarine Tracking Room in London, this episode also demonstrates how effective that tracking room had been during the last few months when convoys were faced with wolf packs of gigantic proportions. The main problem within this centre was that its main brain, that of Commander Rodger Winn, had been absent on sick leave for four weeks, leaving his deputy, Patrick Beesly, to draw conclusions from a mass of often seemingly insignificant signals flooding in. To make matters worse, there was also a serious problem in Britain with either the radio interception stations or with the deciphering process. For inexplicable reasons, the Submarine Tracking Room did not receive the first U-boat sighting report. This had hardly been made when an American aircraft spotted and attacked *U124* (Kptlt Jochen Mohr) some 20 miles behind the convoy. The message from this aircraft was intercepted by the German radio monitoring service, to give the first indication that a convoy might be on its way.

The signal reporting the sighting of convoy TM1 appeared at the U-boat Command shortly after group *Delphin* had been assembled some 1,000 miles away on the other side of the Atlantic. This is, incidentally, further than the distance between London and Rome and the ships in question were moving (in Dönitz's words) at the speed of a pedal cyclist, so Dönitz's first reaction was to keep group *Delphin* searching along its original course. Later he agreed with his staff officers and diverted the patrol line. However, he still didn't like the proposal and after four days told the group to go back on its original course, meaning it was unlikely to make contact with the tanker convoy. Things appeared to be going well for TM1. Nobody on the Allied side knew that their position had been discovered, thinking the convoy had shaken off the five submarines known to have been operating around its departure port of Trinidad. It was not until *U514* (Kptlt Hans-Jürgen Auffermann) sighted and attacked the convoy, sinking the British tanker *British Vigilance* on 3 January 1943, that Dönitz ordered group *Delphin* to be diverted once more. By this time there was no chance of the patrol line being able to spread out at right-angles across the path of the convoy. In other words, the chances of meeting them were still exceedingly slim, but the knowledge that these were valuable tankers gave Dönitz the impetus to have a go. The astonishing point about this entire plan was that this was taking place while the convoy and the U-boats were still a long distance apart and the recent past had demonstrated quite clearly that convoys had the habit of evaporating rather quickly from the surface of the seas.

It must be added that this was more than a mere convoy operation. The recovery of prestige was also at stake. Germany only learned of Operation Torch, the North African landings, when it was too late to prevent them. Fifteen U-boats were hastily called together, but arrived when it was all over. So finding a convoy made up entirely of tankers, obviously heading for this vital hot spot, meant the stakes were exceedingly high — the loss of that vital fuel would result in grave repercussions on a wide front.

The tankers continued running along their route and even slight variations in their course still brought them slap bang into the middle of the wolf pack, so that it was a simple case of both wings closing around the tankers to sink all but two of them, which finally arrived at Gibraltar on 14 January 1943. In addition to the problems experienced on the intelligence front, the escort group under Commander Boyle had also had a rough time. The destroyer *Havelock* and the corvettes *Godetia*, *Pimpernel* and *Saxifrage* had been in American waters and faced an acute shortage of spare parts for the majority of their technical equipment. Consequently the group was handicapped by the failure of such vital parts such as engines, HF/DF, and its radar sets, just at critical moments when they were required. To make matters even worse, the escorts were painted a standard warship grey instead of the more subtle camouflage patterns devised by the ornithologist, Peter Scott. As a result, U-boats had little difficulty in picking them out, even during dark nights, and therefore avoided themselves being chased away.

Despite this success, the U-boat Command was not resting on its laurels and was still eagerly trying to answer the question as to why and how so many convoys seemed to be avoiding the wolf packs. These questions had climbed high on the list of priorities during the previous summer, and U-boats were later provided with rough wooden crosses, supporting a simple aerial for picking up Allied radar impulses. Known as

the Biscay Cross, this simple device helped many to negotiate what the U-boat men were calling the Black Pit of Biscay. This equipment was in such short supply that many radio operators made their own and some handed it to incoming colleagues once they reached the far extremities of the danger zone. For some time surprise attacks had been blamed on poor lookouts, but this simple device confirmed that there was something far more sinister on the technological front. However, Hitler's previous order to discontinue long-term research projects had lost Germany its vital foothold in this most valuable field.

The success against convoy TM1 tends to overshadow the fact that another 100 or so U-boats were at sea but saw the enemy only when they themselves came under surprise attack. So, all in all, January 1943 turned out to be another disastrous month for Germany. Yet, the steps taken to improve matters were minute when compared to the size of the problem. So far commanders had been told to dive for about 30 minutes or so whenever their radar detector produced a response, indicating enemy activity near them. This had the disadvantage that merchant ships being shadowed had moved on by some four to eight miles and a burst at high speed was required to catch them up again. This was all well and good during favourable conditions, but somewhat difficult during storms, fog or other adverse weather so often thrown up by the raging Atlantic. Now, early in 1943, the U-boat Command suggested that U-boats should avoid the enemy, not by diving but by sailing at right-angles to the anticipated approach. German experts calculated that radar sets would lose contact with the U-boat at around the time it could easily be spotted by lookouts on the surface and from then had to rely on visual sighting to make contact. The reason for this was that the distance between sending the radar impulse and picking up its echo would be too short and the two would appear simultaneously on the receiver screen.

At this stage something rather strange and inexplicable happened. Admiral Dönitz recognised the extreme pressure his crews were being exposed to and asked the Supreme Naval Command to step up U-boat production. Yet, only a few weeks earlier he had acknowledged that the conventional, existing types were obsolete and that completely new types of submarine must be built. What was more, plans for the new Types XXI and XXIII were already under way.

The radar story trickled along with seemingly good results until March 1943 when reports started flooding in of U-boats being attacked without having received any warning from their detectors. By this time the Biscay Cross had been replaced by a more substantial aerial which did not have to be dismantled every time the boat dived and, at first, the U-boat Command blamed these attacks on human failure. It was not until Kptlt Jochen Mohr (*U124*) and Korvkpt Werner Hartenstein (*U156*) produced conclusive evidence to the contrary that Dönitz realised something serious was afoot. Both these boats had French sets with magic eyes. These once common devices have now vanished from the majority of radios. They allowed the set to be finely tuned with the aid of a light beam inside a small glass tube, with the advantage that the operator did not have to listen too carefully to his crackling receiver in order to get the best adjustment. Both commanders and radio operators from these two boats reported that these visible tuners were responding to some inaudible signals, suggesting a new type of transmission was being picked up. Despite these discoveries, it took representations from strong personalities, like 'Ali' Cremer of *U333*, to drive the fact home that the enemy was using some type of radar which could not be heard by the German receivers.

Left: U181 (Korvkpt Kurt Freiwald) approaching Penang in the Far East with extended circular dipole aerial of the radar detector.

Below right: U592 running into St Nazaire with the inscription 'Medical doctor from duty. North Atlantic. Consultations up to sea state 5'. Of special interest is the radar detector to the right of the man with the white jacket. This circular dipole aerial replaced the wooden Biscay Cross and did not have to be dismantled when the boat dived.

Left: The aerial for the High Frequency Direction Finder (HF/DF) or Huff Duff on the top of the mast aboard HMS *Plymouth* at the Warship Preservation Trust in Birkenhead (England). Although earlier models were slightly different, a sailor from World War 2 would recognise this rather typical geometric jumble of rigid wires.

Chapter 16

New Bosses November 1942–February 1943

There was a change in leadership on both sides at roughly the same time. During November 1942, Admiral Sir Percy Noble was replaced as Commander-in-Chief of the Western Approaches by Admiral Max Horton, a submariner from World War 1 and then flag officer at HMS *Dolphin*, the Royal Navy's submarine training establishment. Some historians noted that there was a sharp rise in the number of U-boats sunk shortly after this and therefore heaped the laurels of success upon the new leader, without acknowledging the groundwork completed by his predecessor. The biggest problem had been to find the right spot where depth charges should be dropped. Locating even a slow moving submerged object took a long time and the Royal Navy had been so much under strength that escorts could not be spared to hunt U-boats to destruction. It would have been all too easy to reach a situation where every escort was absent hunting U-boats, whales or other marine life a long way from the convoy while the vulnerable merchant ships were left exposed for a second wave of attackers. Admiral Noble's success must be judged by the fact that the vast majority of U-boats at sea never got within torpedo launching range of the enemy.

Another point worth remembering is that most assessments of the performance of these two men were made at a time when very little was known about the Operational Intelligence Centre in London and nothing at all about the part played by cryptanalysts at Bletchley Park. Today there are some wild estimates that Bletchley Park helped to shorten the war by two years, but, despite this, there still is no detailed evaluation of the role the cryptanalysts played in the destruction of the wolf packs. It also seems strange that very little has been written about Rodger Winn, the head of the Submarine Tracking Room and the brain behind many of the Allied successes.

The change in German leadership was considerably more astonishing than the new face in Liverpool. On 30 January 1943, the U-boat Chief, Admiral Karl Dönitz, was appointed to replace Grand Admiral Raeder as Commander-in-Chief of the German Navy. There were several unusual aspects of this. First, Raeder had held this top post for over 14 years, having been appointed to succeed Admiral Hans Zenker in October 1928, and during that long time in power he did not have a

Below: A reconstruction of Admiral Sir Max Horton's room at the Western Approaches Headquarters in Liverpool with a window overlooking the massive maps in the operations room. The building is now open as a museum to provide a fascinating insight into how this unique establishment functioned.

significant second in command or anyone ready to step into his shoes. This would appear somewhat unusual, especially when one considers that both Zenker and his predecessor, Admiral Paul Behnke, occupied the top position for only four years. Both of them were 54 years old when they took command and Raeder, having been born on 24 April 1876, was almost 67 by the time he resigned. So, he served as Commander-in-Chief at an age when the majority of officers had already retired. Following Hitler's request to name possible successors, Raeder suggested that Admiral Rolf Carls (Commander of Group Command North) would be the most suitable, but that Hitler might prefer Karl Dönitz if he wished to emphasise the importance of the U-boat war.

Today the move to appoint Dönitz looks as if it followed a natural line of progression, but in many ways it was quite revolutionary. To start with, at senior level Dönitz had hardly any experience of how the Supreme Naval Command functioned. In fact, his appointment in 1935 to become chief of the 1st U-boat Flotilla was just as unusual. Many historians have smoothed over the rough edges by saying that he was a submariner of World War 1, but this is highly misleading. Dönitz may have commanded *UC25* and *UB68* during that war, but he can hardly be described as a person with his heart firmly fixed in submarines. The reason he joined the silent service was because there were no other posts available. At that time, Germany was expanding its submarine force and needed every man with the right attributes to join this new arm.

Following World War 1, Dönitz became firmly established as a surface sailor, with the grand ambition of becoming a cruiser squadron commander, but this was frustrated by

political circumstances. The agreement with Britain for Germany to be allowed to rebuild a substantial submarine force came as a surprise to many, including the leadership of the still small Reichsmarine. The naval hierarchy had planned to accommodate their handful of submarines within an existing torpedo boat or destroyer flotilla. The turmoil created by the unexpected expansion due to the Anglo-German Naval Agreement still prevailed when Fregattenkapitän Karl Dönitz's light cruiser *Emden* returned from a world cruise in 1935. Dönitz had already established two brand-new units: first he commissioned a torpedo boat flotilla and then, following a lengthy refit, he brought the *Emden* back into service with a new crew. In addition to this, he was known as a man of vision who could work without having to adhere to the rule book. So in many ways he appeared just at the right time, to fill the vacancy for a U-boat flotilla leader until a more suitable person could be found. This was not easy, but Hans-Georg von Friedeburg, an organisational wizard, was appointed to succeed Dönitz once he (Friedeburg) had learned the intricacies of commanding a submarine. These plans fell flat and the war started before the switch could be made. So von Friedeburg remained as head of the U-boat Arm's Organisation Department, while Dönitz took the few U-boats to war, with Korvkpt Eberhard Godt as his second in command.

Above: Karl Dönitz in jovial mood, teasing a waitress.

Above: Karl Dönitz shortly after having awarded the Knight's Cross of the Iron Cross to Kptlt Herbert Kuppisch of *U94*. Kuppisch later also commanded *U516* and *U847*, which took him to his early death.

Right: KptzS Hans Rösing (FdU — Flag Officer for U-boats: West) on the left and Kptlt Adalbert Schnee (*U6, U60, U121, U201* and *U2511*) wearing new leather coats while walking through the FdU:West compound near Angers in France.

Left: Kptlt Rolf Thomsen of *U1202* shaking hands with KptzS Hans Rösing (FdU:West).

Below: Key members of the U-boat Command: Günter Hessler, Eberhard Godt and Karl Dönitz in their Paris headquarters. Dönitz refused to award Hessler a well earned Knight's Cross for his performance in *U107* because he was his son-in-law and he did not want to be seen giving special privileges to his family. Grand Admiral Erich Raeder (Supreme Commander-in-Chief of the Navy) sent a terse memorandum saying that he would present this medal personally if the U-boat Chief failed to do so. By the time this picture was taken, Hessler had been made staff officer and Godt was Dönitz's deputy in the Operations Room, which had already become known as U-boat Command by the time it moved to Paris.

Above: Admiral Karl Dönitz with KptzS Hans Rösing (FdU:West) behind.

Chapter 17

The Dreadful Spring and Awful Summer February–October 1943

March 1943 has usually been taken as the climax of the Battle of the Atlantic, and May as marking the collapse of the U-boat offensive. Yes, March did see the biggest convoy battle, but it is more than highly questionable whether this was a significant climax. After all, although a large number of U-boats came into contact with two convoys bringing on a bloody battle, their individual performance was quite appalling. On average, U-boats at sea managed to sink less than one ship each. Six months earlier, when the wolf packs first returned to the mid-Atlantic air gap, each boat was managing to sink two ships. So there had been a serious deterioration in overall performance. This certainly did not go unnoticed at the U-boat Command, where Dönitz noted in his diary that the losses must be considered serious for the enemy, but that they were also rather disappointing for the U-boats.

The thought that May 1943 was the turning point of the U-boat offensive has been generated by academics who failed to read Dönitz's log books and study the general statistics. Yes, the U-boat losses rose to staggering proportions. Forty or so were sunk during that fateful black May, but Dönitz looked upon this very much as a temporary setback and quoting this number of 40 or so U-boats lost tends to make one forget that almost half that number were sunk during February, when nothing was supposed to have happened.

The spring of 1943 was certainly a period of extremes. Even today, more than half a century later, it is difficult to extract the necessary information from the log books of both sides to work out how the extremes were achieved. The astonishing part of this whole chain of events is that the biggest convoy battle was fought during March, but yet during the following month convoy HX231 managed to throw off almost every attacking U-boat from the *Löwenherz* group.

Personal information can throw much light on the events but unfortunately all too little of this has ever been recorded. For example, *U377's* last voyage under Kptlt Otto Köhler took the boat right into the middle of that cauldron where so many were lost, but it came home with only superficial damage. The reason was quite simple. Britain was locating U-boats from positions broadcast in code over the radio and Midshipman Fritz Beske, who was responsible for navigation, had made a drastic error of well over 100 miles. Since no one was checking his figures, he decided not to tell anyone and continued cooking the books for a period of several days until his numbers finally tallied with the correct position, and by that time they were almost back home in France. So it is quite likely that Allied units were looking for *U377*, but failed to add it the statistics for Black May 1943. This story would probably have never come to light had Beske not confessed during *U377's* first reunion in 1982.

Dönitz did not throw in the towel after his disastrous losses in May 1943, as many historians have claimed, but instructed the remaining boats to move south, where they formed a patrol line to the south-west of the Azores, under the name of group

Trutz. Once again the lack of coherent intelligence prevented the U-boat Command from appreciating fully the extent of Allied air cover and the fact that many of the aircraft in far flung corners of the ocean came from carriers was not fully realised until later. On this occasion, the United States carrier *Bogue* and a good entourage of escorts were employed to bring *Trutz* to battle. The 45-ship-strong convoy GUS7A was rerouted southwards as a result of Enigma decrypts and then it used its High Frequency Direction Finders to avoid the wolf pack. At the same time *Bogue* launched a series of relentlessly punishing attacks against the patrol line. When the three southernmost boats were bombed in rapid succession, the U-boat Command decided that things were getting too hot and ordered the immediate disbanding of the wolf pack. Once again, the Allies had emphasised their superiority in what had been considered a relatively safe area. This made it quite clear that there was no longer an air gap in the Atlantic and all the U-boat Command could look forward to was the loss of more boats. Yet, despite this desperate situation, there was no way that Dönitz was giving up the struggle. He knew it was only a matter of months before new weapons would provide better chances and he did not want to weaken his pressure on the enemy's lifeblood.

Obviously, continuing with wolf pack operations against convoys in the North Atlantic was suicidal and alternatives had to be found or the entire submarine fleet would have to be laid up until the new weapons were operational. Once again, the slimmest of opportunities provided a solution. Supply boats were appearing in greater numbers, making it possible to send wolf packs into far off waters, where surprise might still be on the German side to provide opportunities before troublesome aircraft made those havens untenable also. The Caribbean, the Florida area, the Amazon estuary, West Africa and the Indian Ocean all came within reach. Unfortunately for the U-boat Command, refuelling positions were being transmitted to boats at sea and Bletchley Park was now well into understanding the four wheel radio code, enabling Britain to pinpoint these vulnerable spots. Since time was thought still to be on the German side, it seemed best to refuel before starting aggressive action in the far flung corners of the earth. The mistaken idea was that surprise attacks could then be followed by a hitch free trek home.

Dönitz also did not know that production lines for Allied aircraft were running so well that Coastal Command could, for the first time, mount a constant surveillance in the Bay of Biscay by flying a continuous patrol chain. This made it exceedingly difficult to get in or out of the French bases. At their Casablanca Conference the Allied leaders agreed to make the fighting of U-boats one of their main objectives and at last Coastal Command and other maritime forces began to get a more reasonable share of resources.

The success of the Allied Bay offensive was due to a combination of factors. First, code-breaking allowed forces to be employed in the most effective areas. Aircraft had been equipped with short wave radar, a type which the German detectors could not pick up; they had powerful Leigh Lights for attacking surfaced U-boats at night and a new type of rocket, more effective in some circumstances than depth charges. It was April 1943 before the U-boat Command finally accepted the existence of short wave airborne radar and from then on focused on it to the exclusion of considering other potential problems like insecure codes.

Finding that aircraft in the Bay of Biscay were the most persistent threat, the U-boat Command ordered boats to cross it in groups with the hope that their combined firepower would deter attackers. At the same time, half a dozen boats were converted into special aircraft traps by providing them with an unusually high number of anti-aircraft guns. Several different designs and combinations were built, but it did not take long to prove that even this increased firepower was no match against fast flying aircraft with armour in front of the vital components. Since hitting the fuselage did not seem to have a great effect, gunners tried aiming for the engines, but these made such small targets from a rolling and pitching base that the effort was

Below: Korvkpt Adolf Cornelius Piening (right) from the Frisian Island of Föhr, seen here as commander of the 7th U-boat Flotilla in St Nazaire talking to Kptlt Horst Kessler of *U985*. Piening brought his heavily damaged *U155* successfully home, against heavy odds, by hogging Spanish territorial waters instead of taking the shortest route through the Bay of Biscay and later had that top secret route named after him.

futile. Aircraft traps had only a short life. It was also quickly realised that the lack of protection for the gun crews almost invariably produced such heavy casualties that the struggle was not worth it even if the boat itself survived. Yet, despite the heavy losses, there were no shortages of volunteers willing to take these death traps to sea.

A similar thing happened in Britain when aircraft were faced with the combined firepower from several boats. Rather than being put off, aircrews started discussing eagerly how they might combat the new threat. If anything, it made them more determined to attack, and this resolve paid dividends in that virtually every U-boat passing through the Bay suffered some type of harassment and the majority were also damaged to some degree. Much of this success was due to close co-operation with surface escort groups, meaning there was no let up for U-boats and operations in far distant waters were becoming a pipe dream.

The Allied onslaught against the wolf packs had forced Dönitz entirely onto the defensive, to such an extent that sinking enemy ships no longer formed the central part of his operational orders. Determined to keep a finger on the pulse, Dönitz dispatched boat after boat to seek out weak points. The next step, after learning that the aircraft traps had failed, was to instruct boats not to cross the Bay of Biscay on the surface. Submerged passages at speeds of two to four knots became the order of the day, meaning it took an eternity to get across the danger zone. Ironically the boats were being provided with impressive and very expensive concrete shelters in their French home ports, but reaching these from sea was becoming increasingly difficult. The sad point for the Germans was that air cover could not be provided, even for damaged boats crawling through the danger zone. Occasionally aircraft did make an appearance to lift morale, but generally boats struggled home against powerful odds to fall foul of uninterrupted air attacks on their own doorstep. Yet, despite the gloom, the idea of remaining submerged the whole time, except to recharge batteries, usually during the last hours of the night, paid excellent dividends. The number of boats attacked was instantly reduced. However, this was in no sense a victory because they were not attacking anything nor achieving any significant offensive results.

During this gloomy time, Germany did find one safe route almost by accident. *U155* (Korvkpt Adolf Piening) crawled back to Lorient with heavy damage by sailing along the Spanish coast. However, passing through territorial waters of a neutral country could bring political repercussions and the path was made known only to U-boat commanders, who were instructed to use it only in dire emergencies. Even then they were told not to surface during daylight so that they would not be spotted by Spaniards going about their daily business.

The problem of becoming easy targets for aircraft was overcome by switching techniques again so that boats travelled on their own with individuals spread over a vast area. This coincided with the first operation into far-off waters, where supply tankers were going to play a vital role. This, of course, meant that operational boats would have to concentrate in one spot and that was the very thing Dönitz was trying to prevent. Any such congregation made matters relatively easy for anyone capable of understanding the secret radio code. Submarine supply boats had been in use for just over a year, since America joined in the war, meaning the fleet had been built from nothing to a force of about 10 to a dozen, including a few operational boats used as tankers. So far, supply operations had been running quite well, without any great loss. Three tankers had been sunk, but this happened either while they were on their way out or on their way back, passing through the vulnerable Black Pit of Biscay. So far the actual supply operations themselves had not come under direct surprise attack because the U-boat Command selected lonely places in out-of-the-way locations which land-based aircraft could not reach and Britain did not break into the new radio code until the end of 1942.

From June 1943 onwards, special hunter-killer groups were dispatched specifically to smash this new supply network. Consequently, only two purpose-built supply boats remained afloat by the end of August, bringing offensive operations in distant waters to an abrupt end. Only special long-range voyages to the Far East continued. The struggle for supply submarines was not given up easily and numerous attempts were made to change the procedures. Initially, standing orders prohibited both surface ships (during earlier days) and U-boats from using their radio or engaging in combat two days either side of a refuelling. The position of the supply source was broadcast and beacon signals were transmitted only if boats did not show at the appointed time. Early in June 1943, this practice was stopped and boats were told to search for the tanker by criss-crossing the rendezvous area. Then, if they did not make contact after a two day search, boats were allowed to ask for brief homing signals. To make matters even more difficult for the enemy, meetings were scheduled for the last two hours before sunset, so that the participating boats could remain submerged during the day and then start the transfer of supplies shortly after dark. Doing this without being able to see properly and with only the meagrest of muffled lighting was indeed a most nerve-racking task. The rendezvous positions were encoded with especially elaborate settings and, in addition to this, a system of disguised numbers was used as well. This made it difficult for Bletchley Park to supply the exact location, but co-operation with the Submarine Tracking Room often made it possible to make reasonable guesses as to where the boats might be.

The first very long-range Type IXD2 boats were commissioned early in 1942 by modifying the design for the standard, ocean-going Type IX. An additional set of cruising engines was added and these were balanced with additional crew accommodation forward of the conning tower. This added length also made it possible to enlarge the tanks running around the outside of the pressure hull, to give the boats an incredible range of over 32,000 nautical miles (60,000 kilometres). The drawback was that many of the fittings were similar to those on the standard Type IX and therefore hydroplane responses were less effective. Keeping the extra length at periscope depth was almost impossible without the bows or stern breaking through the surface of the water. This made these larger boats far too clumsy for use in the convoy battles of the North Atlantic.

The *Seehund* group was active in the Indian Ocean from February to April 1943, at a time when Dönitz still had considerable reservations about sending boats to such far-off waters. He was not thinking so much of the sinkings the few boats might achieve, but the panic they could create and the forces they might tie up a long way from home. Incidentally, neither the *Seehund* pack nor the later groups operating in the Indian Ocean functioned as a patrol line. Each boat was very much on its own and usually only made contact with the others in cases of emergency or to refuel from the same supply source.

With the change in the general situation and with the North Atlantic having become untenable for ordinary U-boats, the Indian Ocean was looked upon in a different light and definite plans were made to send a wolf pack there. The idea was that they might refuel at a Japanese base and then come home as cargo carriers with valuable raw materials aboard. All these developments took place incredibly fast, making it impossible to make proper preparations, and communication with the Japanese was not easy at the best of times. It was very much a case of sending some boats to explore the possibilities. The men in *U178* (Korvkpt Wilhelm Dommes) were looking forward to their homeward-bound journey from the Indian Ocean when Dönitz asked whether it was possible to reach the Far East.

Below: Pictures like this one have appeared in many books, but these special aircraft traps were used for only a short period and photographs of them are exceedingly rare. This shows *U441* under Kptlt Götz von Hartmann with what Germany thought was enough firepower to shoot down Coastal Command aircraft. All this effort showed was that the Royal Air Force had far superior guns and the undersized U-boat weapons could contribute only towards their own serious losses. The rotatable bedstead type of aerial on the top of the conning tower had a radar detector on one side and a search device on the other.

Dommes said 'Yes' and instead of going home, he found himself heading off into the unexpected.

In any case, the first thrust into southern waters, group *Monsun*, did not get off to a good start. The supply boat, *U462* (Kptlt Bruno Vowe), got only as far as the western extremities of the Bay of Biscay, when it was so severely damaged by aircraft that it had to return. The only other available supply boat had already been at sea for some time and was therefore not in a position to support the outward-bound group. Therefore, Dönitz had no alternative other than the highly unpopular move of ordering one boat from the group to sacrifice its fuel so that the rest could continue. To make matters awkward, this boat (*U533* under Kptlt Helmut Hennig) had already been sunk meaning that more confusion reigned before the *Monsun* boats could continue with their journeys. While all this was going on, the Allies dispatched a hunter-killer group to the southern waters, making it a miracle that not all the boats were annihilated.

Left: Kptlt Götz von Hartmann (*U555*, *U563* and the aircraft trap *U441*) sporting the type of headgear worn by men aboard the aircraft traps. Just to confuse historians, *U441* was commanded by Kptlt Klaus Hartmann before and after Götz.

Below: Probably *U889* under Kptlt Friedrich Braeucker, showing the later conning tower development with increased anti-aircraft guns. It looks as if the anti-aircraft armament consists of a 37mm and two 20mm twins. The circular radio direction finder aerial, for determining the direction from which radio signals are coming, can be seen towards the left.

Above: U978 under Kptlt Günther Pulst running into Trondheim (Norway) just two weeks before the end of the war. The twin 20mm and single 37mm anti-aircraft guns are clearly visible. The shields on the upper platform were not fitted to all boats and many went to sea without protection for the gun crews.

Right: Probably *U889* under Kptlt Friedrich Braeucker, showing quite clearly that the boat was fitted with one of the new 37mm twins. These proved quite effective against large Coastal Command aircraft, but appeared too late and were fitted to only a few of the larger boats.

Left: U1023 under Kptlt Heinrich Schroeteler in Weymouth shortly after the end of the war. The anti-aircraft armament consists of two 20mm twins and a single 37mm automatic.

Below: U333 under Kptlt 'Ali' Cremer on 26 May 1942 with the new, improved anti-aircraft armament. The 20mm is without any form of protection for the gun crew. The top of the rectangular ventilation shaft has also been modified to accommodate several hydrogen cylinders for filling radar foxer balloons. The men are supporting themselves against the periscope housing and the torpedo sight can be seen behind the man on the left. The slot for the retractable radio direction finder aerial is also visible in the top left edge of the tower.

Chapter 18
U–boats Try Again August–October 1943

Before going on to the convoy battles of autumn 1943, it is necessary to look at a drastic escalation of the air war, which had a profound effect on the Germans at the time, but has almost been forgotten today. To appreciate this, one needs to remember that then events were not so neatly compartmentalised as the presentation of statistics would lead us to believe these days. Thus the gravity of the losses during Black May did not hit home to ordinary German people until some time later, when those boats failed to return. Then officials were faced with the daunting task of informing the crews' next of kin and Dönitz's policy had already established the procedure that U-boat families should be faced not with anonymous official telegrams but personal communications. In the case of lost boats, it fell to flotilla commanders to send out letters, consisting of a closely typed A4 sheet, to explain what had happened, to express their condolences and promise to forward any more information when, and if, it became available. These letters were usually written several weeks after the last day when the boat could have come home because there had been plenty incidents when people had been declared as missing, suddenly to reappear, having been unable to communicate because of a broken radio.

The disasters of Black May turned into such a frightful summer that flotilla chiefs had to find additional secretarial staff to cope with the more than 2,000 letters which had to be sent out. These dreadful losses were still being digested when the bombing campaign against Germany escalated to unimaginably huge proportions, including the creation of a firestorm in one raid against Hamburg which killed an estimated 42,000 people. The result of this human massacre in Germany was that there was nothing the population could do, other than work harder for the war effort. Consequently, these devastating raids helped to increase the rate at which U-boats were being built and the new acoustic torpedoes appeared several months ahead of schedule. This made it possible to prepare a large-scale return to the shipping lanes of the North Atlantic for early September 1943. The plan was that group *Leuthen* should assemble in the danger area between Britain and Canada, where they were going to surprise the Allies with new weapons and new tactics. Commanders were told to dive as soon as their new Hagenuk radar detectors produced a response so that they should be below the surface before an enemy was close enough to detect an echo on his radar set. Thus, in theory, it should be possible to assemble around the convoy without being noticed. Once everybody was in position, the senior officer would give the order, 'Remain on the surface,' which was the instruction for all boats to attack at once. The strengthened AA armament would tackle patrolling aircraft, while the new acoustic torpedo would sink any approaching escorts. There was no standard configuration for the guns, but the general arrangement consisted of two twin 20mm guns plus either a quadruple 20mm or a single 37mm anti-aircraft gun. Yet, even these proved inadequate, though Germany did not discover that until later. Having eliminated the escorts, U-boats were then to use the new anti-convoy torpedoes to tackle the merchant ships.

In addition to the other technical innovations, every boat carried a number of hydrogen bottles for filling balloons carrying metal foil as radar foxers. The idea was that a large number of these should drift some distance behind boats to distract the enemy.

As with all German plans of the time, everything became a case of crisis management. Some boats had not been fitted with the increased anti-aircraft armament and a shortage of acoustic torpedoes meant that these could be carried only by the first wave. Despite these new aids, life in U-boats had become considerably more precarious. Additional guns meant that more men had to be accommodated on the top of the conning tower, which resulted in a noticeable increase in the time it took to dive. Another snag was that all the heavy hardware increased drag and therefore reduced underwater speed, making it more difficult to evade escorts just at that critical moment when they were dropping depth charges. Stability problems were even more serious, meaning that rearrangements of ballast were necessary, but even then the boats were nowhere near as easy to control as the earlier versions and the men were given little or no experience in doing so.

Today it is in vogue never to say anything positive about the Third Reich and films give the impression that the majority of its leaders were cold-blooded morons or thugs without ability. Yet, anyone watching original footage of the famous rallies must be impressed by the feeling of nationalism projected at the time. Recently at least one U-boat commander has written in his autobiography that he was not impressed by Hitler or by the National Socialists, which hardly rings true. There appear to be far more people who would agree with 'Ajax' Bleichrodt when he said that politics had never been his strong point and he did not take a great deal of interest in the government. However, Bleichrodt also said that the day he met Hitler made a profound impression on him and made him realise that his small part in the navy was being fully appreciated by his leaders. Ursula von Friedeburg, the wife of Admiral von Friedeburg, who knew Hitler personally, said that he projected a powerful image of confidence. Dönitz too, was the type of person one did not argue with for the simple reason that he was always ready to listen to his men. That is not to say that the relationship between him and his commanders was completely harmonious. Debriefings often resulted in harsh and bitter criticisms. Yet, Dönitz knew how to get the best out of people. The support and encouragement he supplied shortly before group *Leuthen* departed worked wonders to get the new campaign off the ground. The name may mean virtually nothing to young Germans today, but as one of the victorious battles of Frederick the Great it featured strongly in the history lessons of the Third Reich. Dönitz then sent his men to battle with the words, 'The Führer will follow every phase of your fight. Attack! At them! Sink them!'

Group *Leuthen* was in luck in that most of the boats reached their destination on 20 September 1943 and then quickly made contact with convoy ON202, which then joined forces with the slower ONS18. Initial reports flooding back to base were rather encouraging: the first attack supposedly resulted in seven destroyers definitely and three probably sunk, plus up to three 5,000-ton ships sunk as well. Air attacks on U-boats were relentless, but contact was maintained for another onslaught

Above: The 'Red Devil' boat, *U552* coming into port with a good number of success pennants fluttering from the extended periscope. The snorting bull emblem near the gun platform indicates that the boat belonged to the 7th U-Flotilla in St Nazaire. The commanders were Erich Topp, Klaus Popp and Günther Lube. Topp was one of only five U-boat commanders who were awarded the Knight's Cross with Oakleaves and Swords.

of August or at the beginning of September 1943. The other two lost boats, *U610* and *U336*, can be said to have been very experienced, but the skill and efficiency acquired during earlier voyages did not stand the men in good enough stead when it came to dealing with well-armed, fast-flying aircraft. This convoy battle was still raging out in the Atlantic when the B-Dienst decoded a series of emergency route alterations broadcast to a group of stragglers behind convoy ON204. At first it was assumed that this came about as a result of the first sighting reports by the wolf pack, but quickly it became apparent that these orders were issued before the *Rossbach* group had made contact. Consequently the U-boat Command was presented with spine-chilling evidence that something out of the ordinary was afoot and an inquiry was established to find out how the boats could have been detected. News that *Rossbach* had been discovered came totally out of the blue, especially after the initial success of *Leuthen*, where boats had no problem in positioning themselves in the most advantageous position ahead of the convoy. At the inquiry, Dönitz decided that it might be possible for enemy aircraft to have established the position of the patrol line with their centimetric radar, which U-boats could not yet detect, but he also wrote that it could have come about as a result of treachery from Italian sources.

Short-wave or centimetric radar had been thought as being impossible until April 1943, but it was not until much later in

the summer that German scientists managed to reconstruct a set captured from a crashed bomber near Rotterdam earlier in the year. When its unexpected perfection surprised German leaders they took it to be almost a messenger from hell and immediately blamed the shortcomings of recent times on this wonder device. Sadly, it made them concentrate on centimetric radar being the culprit they were looking for, without studying in detail the other possible contributory causes for their poor achievements.

The Allies had invaded mainland Italy on 3 September 1943, just as *Leuthen* was assembling in mid-Atlantic, and the Italians had surrendered on the 8th. It seemed highly likely that many German secrets had been eagerly handed over to the Allies, including the information that Germany was constantly breaking British ciphers. Whatever might have happened, the U-boat Command had to continue the Atlantic battles effectively. This was not easy, since the answer did not lie within the jurisdiction of the U-boat Arm. The main problem in all convoy battles had been finding the merchant ships. Ideally, their route had to be known some time in advance, so that the pack could assemble in the most advantageous position. The answer was thought to lie with reconnaissance aircraft and Dönitz desperately wanted a large number patrolling the convoy routes.

The success of the Blitzkrieg, especially the speed at which German forces moved through Poland, the Low Countries, France and later Russia, has tended to hide the fact that there were bitter rivalries between the leaders of the German armed forces and these became even worse as the war progressed. Even now, after four years of war in the Atlantic, no one had given the U-boats the air support they so desperately needed. Even damaged boats, crawling home from bitter action, were often left to their own devices to negotiate the dangerous Black Pit of Biscay without any form of support. Only rarely was it possible to provide the necessary cover to prevent the RAF from finishing them off on their own doorstep. Dönitz wanted sufficient aircraft in the Atlantic to guide U-boats to their targets, but he was told that there was not only a shortage of aircraft but also a conspicuous absence of the right type of long-range reconnaissance bombers needed to fly over such vast stretches of water. To make matters even worse, shortly after the failure of *Rossbach*, when some limited air reconnaissance was provided, it was discovered that the crews were not adequately trained to cope with naval warfare. They tended to overestimate the speed of convoys and underestimate the number of escorts. Consequently, U-boats were sent to the wrong areas and if they did make contact, they were often surprised by far more Allied warships than they had expected.

In view of these shortcomings, every available U-boat was sent to sea to help form the next reconnaissance line, including some boats which were hardly seaworthy. The Radio Monitoring Service was working overtime in its land bases and also sent experts to sea aboard the U-boats to listen in to the very high frequency radio transmissions from ships within the convoy to get possible clues as to what was going on and the nature of the transmissions. VHF radio now forms an integral part of modern radio communications, but this was still very much in its infancy during the war and such equipment was not yet universal. One advantage or drawback with it, depending on how one looks at the problem, was that the signals travelled in a line of sight. Therefore a receiver further along the curvature of the earth could not pick up the signals and no matter how high the transmitting aerial might be, one could not hear these broadcasts more than a few dozen miles away. Admittedly the messages were often in plain speech, but with much use of code words and naval slang which made it difficult for an outsider to follow the conversation.

The main conclusion drawn from these trials was that U-boats were wholly inadequate for finding convoys. The raw information for drawing such a conclusion was still passing through the minds of the U-boat Command officers as isolated pieces of evidence and the real underlying reasons had not yet been fully understood when the next set of boats was heading into the danger zone. They desperately needed orders to form a new wolf pack. Named *Schlieffen*, this assembled with 13 boats to head off convoys ON206 and ONS20. As before, this was a case of a fast convoy running behind a slower one so that their escorts could be combined in the critical areas to provide maximum protection. By the time the U-boats had got into position, it was obvious that the mid-Atlantic air gap no longer existed. *U426* (Kptlt Christian Reich), on its first operational patrol, was lucky in sinking one straggler, the British steamer *Essex Lance*, but apart from that the other boats saw nothing but empty seas while having to put up with an abundance of air attacks. Six boats were lost in rapid succession, forcing Dönitz to say that this had been the worst setback of the U-boat war.

It was now clear that the new 20mm anti-aircraft guns were no match for modern fast flying and heavily armed bombers. Far too often the unprotected gun crews found themselves under a hail of shells before they could train their guns on the aircraft. Aiming the quadruple 20mm gun from a constantly rolling and pitching platform, by turning two hand-wheels, was exceedingly tricky. The deck was often slippery as well and the men were nearly always soaking wet, with spray and waves washing around them. The approaching aircraft, on the other hand, could often settle into a comfortable flightpath to aim its superior armament at the exposed U-boat.

Group *Schlieffen* also proved that it was now impossible for U-boats to remain on the surface during the hours of daylight, meaning that drastic changes were more than necessary if the entire fleet was not going to be annihilated. Yet, a few weeks earlier, *Leuthen* was thought to have been such an unqualified success that the U-boat Command was grasping at every opportunity to attempt a repeat of this performance.

For the time being, no one came up with any sensible suggestions about what to do with the next pack, leaving the U-boat Command with no alternative other than to prohibit all daytime activities on the surface. Even the patrol line had to remain submerged if it was going to survive, and this was an incredible drawback, but there was no alternative other than to vacate the shipping lanes altogether. By this time, Hitler appreciated the role which the U-boat Arm was playing and the sacrifices the men were making, and therefore told Dönitz that it was Germany's most important weapon. Judging from the morale within the U-boat Arm, it would seem highly unlikely that the men themselves would have vacated their duties, even if the Führer had suggested it. Dönitz felt it was important to keep in touch with developments at sea and therefore made plans for more convoy battles, but he never managed to re-establish another even vaguely successful force in the North Atlantic and *Schlieffen* was the last wolf pack in the shipping lanes between Britain and Canada.

The *Siegfried* group formed on 24 October in the old style, but in a new location further south, towards the Azores, where fewer aircraft were expected. The orders were to submerge during the day and surface only at night, but this time the B-Dienst failed to obtain any decent intercepts or any clue of a convoy, and HX263 skirted around the southern end of the patrol line. Several other wolf packs were formed after this, but all of them failed to converge on their targets, never mind inflict even any damage on merchant ships. Time and again a new pack was formed after the previous one had been unsuccessful and then suffered even worse casualties. To make matters more difficult, boats were now operating in the southern reaches of the North Atlantic where they required supply boats. A year earlier it was still possible to travel there and back at the most economical speed, but now night-time spurts at high, fuel-guzzling speeds were the usual practice. On 15 November 1943 Dönitz noted that the fuel consumption of the *Eisenhart* group had been exceptionally high, due to the fact that they remained submerged during the day and therefore had to run much faster during the night if they were going to make any decent headway at all. Yet, all the additional sacrifice did not pay dividends and what remained of the pack came home empty handed. The interesting point about these

Above: U534 at the Warship Preservation Trust in Birkenhead with one of the rare 37mm twin anti-aircraft guns.

failures, which has often been omitted from general histories of the war, is that this was happening in November 1943 and the war did not stop until May 1945. This meant that there was another year and a half to go.

The situation is best summed up by a passage from the U-boat Command's war diary which states:

> 'The enemy has all the trumps: long-range aircraft constantly cover all areas and use methods of location against which we still have no sure means of warning. As a result the enemy discovers the positions of our boats and either diverts his convoys away from our U-boats or scatters his traffic over the vastness of the ocean. Our side is still without effective air reconnaissance. The U-boat has to be its own scout, although visibility from the conning tower is not great. We have no means of locating the enemy and boats are now reduced to moving very little because danger from aircraft compels them to remain constantly submerged during the hours of daylight. The enemy sees all our cards and we do not see his, but we really need to know what he is holding if we are going to conduct a successful campaign. We drastically need our own long-range reconnaissance aircraft, if we are going to make any headway in this battle.'

However, despite these drawbacks, there could be no question about withdrawing from the Atlantic. Under the impression that hundreds of aircraft were patrolling every part of the ocean, Dönitz feared that a massive force would be unleashed against German civilians if Coastal Command discovered there were no more U-boats at sea. Yet, although increasing in size and now bigger than ever before, Coastal Command was still nowhere near as large as the Germans had imagined. The reason was simple: the Command was given pretty accurate information about the location of U-boats, and therefore needed to patrol only those critical areas.

The next step was to supplement the patrol line formation with a number of single scouts a long way ahead of the rest of the pack with the sole intention of providing reconnaissance information about the nature of escorts and air support. At the same time, the rest of the pack was divided into a number of small groups of no more than three or four boats side by side. The idea was that some groups should be ahead of the others, making it more difficult for the Allied commanders to guess the location of the pack once they had discovered one or two boats. All this proved was that convoys were somehow avoiding wolf packs and the U-boats' anti-aircraft guns were ineffective. Although the 20mm anti-aircraft guns, both in double and quadruple barrel versions, were considered to be fully functional, they were not powerful enough to deal with the large aircraft now appearing in ever-increasing numbers. Yet, despite this, there were surprising individual success, such as U763 (Kptlt Ernst Cordes) shooting down two aircraft in close succession. On the whole, however, it was decided that it was best to postpone the next *Leuthen* type of attack until all participating boats could be equipped with the new automatic, 37mm anti-aircraft gun. This, incidentally, should not be confused with the earlier 37mm quick-firing deck gun, whose shells had to be fed individually into the breech.

Above: U862, under KptIt Heinrich Timm, one the massive long-range Type IXD2 boats. Both the attack periscope with the small lens and the navigation periscope with the larger head are visible. The large rectangular cavity in the left conning tower wall houses a Type Hohentwiel radar aerial and the circular hole for the extendable rod aerial is visible forward of it. Note that although stronger anti-aircraft guns have been fitted, the large 105mm deck gun has not been removed because it was thought that a use might be found for it in far distant waters.

There was also another novel innovation in the pipeline, but it is now exceedingly difficult to work out the exact details. According to the U-boat Command's War Diary of 22 February 1944, *U906* was the first boat to leave Germany with a set of anti-aircraft rockets on the upper platform of the conning tower, but most records show *U906* not being launched until the end of June 1944, four months after this date.

Several wolf packs were formed during the last weeks of 1943 and the first days of the new year. The common feature running through the comments in the U-boat Command's diary was that none of them made contact with any shipping. On 7 January 1944 Dönitz wrote, 'This means the end of the tactics which we have used so far. Operations against convoys have proved beyond doubt that the opposition's radar has been used to avoid our patrol lines.'

As earlier in the war there were various unexplained incidents around this time. Even Konteradmiral Godt, head of U-boat Operations, could throw no light on the matter when he was asked in the late 1980s about some of these. For example, there is a most fascinating entry in the log for 15 January 1944: 'An Emergency War Report (SOS) was received today saying that a U-boat was seriously damaged after having been hit by a torpedo. It is possible that this has come from one of our own boats, but that is unlikely since a submarine would sink straight away once it has been hit by a torpedo. The message stopped abruptly and there was no signature.' It would seem that this signal added so much confusion that it was pushed aside to be completely ignored and only the Operational Intelligence Centre in London, eager for news about the acoustic torpedo, made inquiries about who could have shot the torpedo at a U-boat which could only have been *U377*. It didn't take long to establish that none of the Allied forces had fired torpedoes. That left the only possibility that another U-boat had been responsible, but this too was impossible. By this time the Operational Intelligence Centre knew more about U-boat dispositions than the U-boat Command and could therefore determine that the next boat in the *Rügen* patrol line was too far away. The other mystery is why was the U-boat Command surprised that the message stopped abruptly? Would that not have been likely if the boat was sinking? The strange point about the SOS was that it was transmitted in the right code and on the right radio frequency. Therefore, assuming that it had not come from a German source then whoever sent it must have had knowledge of the German radio code. Somehow this thought was not considered at the time.

Allowing a little personal digression here, it might be interesting to add that, many years after the war, I received a letter from an Australian pilot saying he might have sunk *U377*, with my father on board on 15 January 1944. This was not the first of such claims, but Wes Loney was different in that he also supplied a copy from his flying log with exact details. He had indeed attacked a U-boat around the time this strange SOS could have been transmitted. A close look at the U-boat Command's war diary indicated a severe air attack on *U552* (Kptlt Klaus Popp), very close to *U377*, at exactly the time given by Wes Loney. *U552* received a hell of a battering, but Wes didn't sink it. It struggled back to France and many years later Wes was able to join the survivors for a reunion in Germany.

U-boat wolf packs continued for the first months of 1944, but the sole reward brought in by this great effort and sacrifice was more confirmation that it was not possible to establish patrol lines. The only result was heavy punishment from aircraft and escorts. The majority never got close enough to aim torpedoes at merchant ships, but those that returned could relate horrific stories of how they were attacked by aircraft without a great deal of warning. The great lesson learned during many months of excruciating hardship was that the wolf pack technique did not work and the only way to achieve even meagre results was for U-boats to operate individually. There was no alternative but to continue with single operations until the new electro-boats arrived to bring about a reversal of fortunes, but they did not appear in time. Germany had already lost the Battle of the Atlantic.

The Main Atlantic and British Coastal Convoy Routes

CODE	ROUTE	COMMENTS
AS	USA–Africa	Started early 1942, mainly military transports
AT	New York–UK	Military transports
CF	Cape Town–UK	
CT	UK–Canada and USA	
CU	Caribbean–UK	Tankers
EBC	English Channel	
ET	Africa–Gibraltar	Started towards the end of 1942
EN	Scotland	Coastal convoys started in the summer of 1940
FN	Southend–Scotland	
FS	Scotland–Southend	
GAT	Guantanamo–Trinidad	
GU	Africa–USA	Mainly military transports, introduced when USA joined the war
GUS	Gibraltar–UK	
HG	Gibraltar–UK	
HX	Halifax (Nova Scotia)–UK	Started in September 1939 for fast ships crossing the North Atlantic
HXF	Halifax (Nova Scotia)–UK	Fast convoys
JW	Loch Ewe in Scotland–Russia	Replaced the PQ convoys towards the end of 1942
KJ	Kingston, Jamaica–UK	
KMF & KMS	UK–Africa UK–Mediterranean–Slow	Carried mainly military materials for Operation Torch, the landings in North Africa
KN	American coastal convoys	
MKF & MKS	North Africa–UK	Started towards the end of 1942
NA	North America–UK	Fast military transports
OB	UK–North America	
OG	UK–Gibraltar	
ON	UK–North America	Started in the summer of 1941 to replace OB
ONS	UK–North America	ON slow
OS	UK–Africa	
PQ	Iceland–Russia	Later became known as JW
QP	North Russia–Iceland	
RA	Russia–Scotland	
RS	Gibraltar southwards	
RU	Reykjavik, Iceland–UK	
SC	Halifax (Nova Scotia) / New York–UK	Consisted mainly of slower merchant ships
SG	Sydney, Nova Scotia–Greenland	
SH	Sydney–Halifax	
SL	Sierra Leone–UK	
SR	Sierra Leone–Gibraltar	
TM	Trinidad–Gibraltar	Tanker convoys
TO	Africa–America	Fast tankers
TU	UK–America	Started running in the autumn of 1943
UC	UK–America / Caribbean	Tanker convoys
UGF	USA to Gibraltar	
UGS	USA to Gibraltar	
UR	UK to Iceland	
US	Australia to Suez	US3 was diverted to UK
UT	America–UK	
WS	UK–southwards	
XK	Gibraltar–UK	

The Major U-Boat Wolf Packs

The date column indicates roughly the day when the group was formed or first thought of. Some packs did not assemble until several days after this date.

DATE	NAME OF U-BOAT GROUP	AREA/CONVOY ATTACKED	U-BOATS (THE 'U' PREFIX HAS BEEN OMITTED)
1939			
01.10	First wolf pack attempt	not established	37, 40, 42, 45, 46, 48
06.11	Second wolf pack attempt	not established	38, 41, 43, 47, 49
1940			
14.03		Against British Submarines	7, 9, 12, 19, 20, 24, 56, 57, 59
18.03		West of Orkney	38, 43, 44, 47, 49
12.06	Prien	HX48	25, 28, 30, 32, 38, 47, 51
12.06	Rösing	US3	29, 43, 46, 48, 101
15.06	E-W Patrol Line	North Channel	25, 28, 30, 32, 47, 51, 65
17.06	E-W Patrol Line	Western Channel	29, 43, 46, 48, 101
02.09	First successful group attack	SC2	28, 47, 65, 99, 101, 124
20.09		HX72	29, 32, 43, 46, 47, 48, 65, 99, 100
09.10			37, 38, 48, 103, 123
17.10		SC7	38, 46, 48, 99, 100, 101, 123
19.10		HX79	28, 38, 46, 47, 48, 100
08.11		HX84, SC11	47, 93, 100, 103, 104, 123, 137, 138
03.12		SC13	34, 52, 94, 99, 103
1941			
29.01		SC19	52, 93, 94, 101, 103, 106
03.02		OB279	52, 96, 103, 123
19.02		OB287	48, 69, 73, 96, 107
22.02		OB287	69, 73, 96, 97, 107, 552
25.02		OB290	47, 73, 97, 99
06.03		OB293	A, 47, 70, 74, 99
15.03		HX112	37, 74, 99, 100, 110
25.03		HX115, SC26	46, 48, 69, 73, 74, 76, 97, 98, 101
18.04		South of Iceland	73, 101, 110
28.04		HX121	65, 95, 96, 123, 552
09.05	West		20, 74, 93, 94, 97, 98, 109, 111, 556
15.05	West		74, 93, 94, 97, 98, 109, 111, 556
25.05	Bismarck	Escort for battleship *Bismarck*	43, 46, 66, 94, 557. 48, 97, 98, 556 on way home. 73 on way out.
01.06	West	Loose formation	43, 46, 66, 73, 75, 77, 93, 101, 108, 204, 553, 557, 558, 751
20.06		Loose formation	43, 71, 75, 77, 79, 96, 101, 108, 111, 201, 202, 203, 271, 553, 556, 557
24.06		HX133	71, 79, 201, 203, 371, 552, 556, 562, 564, 651
29.06		OG66	77, 96, 98, 108, 111, 201, 202, 553, 557, 559, 561, 562, 564
15.07		OG69, SL80	68, 74, 95, 97, 98, 126, 203, 331, 372, 401, 431, 561, 562, 564, 565
24.07		OG69, SL80	68, 79, 126, 203, 331, 561, 562, 564

DATE	NAME OF U-BOAT GROUP	AREA/CONVOY ATTACKED	U-BOATS (THE 'U' PREFIX HAS BEEN OMITTED)
1941			
30.07		SL81	46, 74, 75, 83, 97, 204, 205, 372, 401, 431, 558, 559, 565
06.08		HG68	43, 46, 71, 75, 83, 96, 204, 205, 372, 559, 751
09.08		HG69	79, 93, 94, 109, 123, 124, 126, 331, 371
10.08		SL81	75, 83, 106, 201, 204, 552, 559, 564
22.08		OS4, ON12	83, 95, 101, 141, 143, 557, 561, 751
28.08	Markgraf	SC42, HX146, HX147, ON	38, 81, 82, 84, 85, 105, 202, 207, 432, 433, 501, 569, 652
01.09	Kurfürst	OG73	77, 96, 206, 553, 563, 567, 568
01.09	Bosemüller	SL84	71, 83, 95, 557, 558, 561, 562, 751
02.09	Seewolf	OG73, HG72, SC42	Combined Kurfürst and Bosemüller
15.09	Brandenburg	ON14, SC44	69, 74, 94, 372, 373, 552, 562, 572, 575
17.09	Goeben	First group to move into the Mediterranean	75, 79, 97, 331, 371, 559
02.10	Breslau	OG75, HG74, HG75	71, 83, 204, 206, 563, 564
09.10		ONS23, SC48, ONS24, ONS25	101, 109, 208, 374, 432, 502, 553, 558, 568, 573
18.10	Reissewolf	SC50, ON28	73, 77, 101, 106, 432, 502, 568, 751 (?)
20.10	Mordbrenner	ONS27	109, 208, 374, 573
28.10	Schlagetot	SL89, HX155	38, 82, 84, 85, 93, 123, 202, 203, 569
30.10	Stosstrupp		96, 133, 552, 567, 571, 577
01.11	Störtebecker	HG75, HG76, OS11	69, 85, 96, 98, 103, 107, 133, 201, 373, 571, 572, 577
08.11	Raubritter	SC52, SC53, OS11	38, 82, 85, 106, 123, 133, 571, 577
09.11		Various groups moving into Mediterranean over a period of time	43, 74, 77, 81, 83, 95, 133, 202, 205, 206, 208, 372, 374, 375, 432, 433, 451, 453, 557, 558, 562, 565, 568, 569, 573, 577
19.11	Gödecke	OG77	96, 332, 402, 552
19.11	Benecke	OG77	96, 332, 402, 552
19.11	Steuben		67, 105, 372, 434, 574, 575
22.11		Loose group in South Atlantic used mainly to rescue survivors from Atlantis and Python	A, 68, 124, 126, 129
26.11	Letzter Ritter	OG77	69, 201, 402
14.12	Seeräuber	HG76	67, 107, 108, 131, 434
25.12	Ulan	PQ7, PQ8	134, 454, 584
27.12	Paukenschlag	USA	66, 109, 123, 125, 130. This was not a wolf pack but an operation.
1942			
08.01	Ziethen		84, 86, 87, 135, 203, 333, 552, 553, 582, 654, 701, 754
11.01	Seydlitz	HG78	71, 93, 571
14.01	Schlei	Defence of Norway	
21.01	2nd Wave	USA	103, 106, 107, 108, 128
16.02	Neuland	First wave to Caribbean	67, 126, 129, 156, 161, 502
		Second wave to Caribbean	126 — only one boat
00.02		Hebrides - Faeroes	136, 213, 352, 455, 591, 653, 752
00.03		Hebrides - Faeroes	87, 135, 553, 569, 593, 701, 753
11.05	Hecht	ONS92, ONS93, ONS94, ONS96, ONS100, ONS102	94, 96, 124, 406, 569, 590. First self-contained pack with supply submarine (U116)
14.05	Endrass	HG84	84, 89, 132, 134, 437, 552, 571, 675
21.05	Pfadfinder	E of America	135, 213, 404, 432, 455, 553, 566, 578, 653
01.07	Eisteufel	PQ17	88, 251, 255, 334, 355, 376, 408, 456, 457, 657
11.07	Hai	OS33	116, 136, 201, 572, 582, 752
12.07	Wolf	ON111, ON113, ON115	43, 71, 86, 379, 454, 552, 597, 704

DATE	NAME OF U-BOAT GROUP	AREA/CONVOY ATTACKED	U-BOATS (THE 'U' PREFIX HAS BEEN OMITTED)
1942			
01.08	Lohs	SC95, ONS122, SC100	135, 174, 176, 256, 373, 432, 438, 569, 596, 605, 660, 705, 755
01.08	Pirat	ON115	42, 71, 164, 210, 217, 454, 511, 552, 553, 597, 607, 704
03.08	Steinbrink	SC94	71, 174, 176, 210, 256, 379, 438, 454, 593, 595, 597, 605, 607, 660, 704, 705
17.08	Blücher	SL118, SL119	214, 333, 406, 566, 590, 594
20.08	Iltis	SL119	107, 214, 406, 566
23.08	Eisbär	SL119	68, 156, 172, 504
24.08	Stier	SC97	Outward-bound boats became Vorwärts
27.08	Vorwärts	SC97, ONS127	91, 92, 211, 407, 409, 411, 604, 609, 659, 756
04.09	Vorwärts 2	ONS127, SC100	91, 92, 96, 211, 218, 380, 404, 411, 584, 594, 608, 659
06.09	Lohs	SC100	135, 176, 259, 373, 410, 432, 569, 599, 755
08.09	Pfeil	SC99, SC100, ON129	176, 216, 221, 258, 356, 373, 410, 569, 595, 599, 607, 615, 617, 618, 755
10.09	Tiger	ON131	176, 216, 221, 258, 356, 373, 410, 569, 599, 607, 615, 617, 618, 755
16.09	Vorwärts 3	RB1, SC100	91, 96, 211, 260, 380, 404, 407, 582, 584, 619
30.09	Luchs	HX209	183, 254, 257, 260, 382, 437, 442, 582, 597, 602, 610, 619, 620, 706, 753, 757
01.10	Tümmler		Transit group to Mediterranean
08.10	Panther	ON137, ON139, ONS136, ONS148, SC104	84, 254, 260, 301, 353, 382, 437, 441, 442, 443, 454, 563, 575, 597, 602, 610, 620, 621, 621, 662, 706, 753, 757
08.10	Wotan	ON135, ONS136, SC104	71, 84, 89, 132, 216, 356, 381, 402, 438, 454, 571, 609, 568, 661
14.10	Leopard	ONS136, ONS137, ONS138, ONS139, SC104	221, 258, 356, 410, 599, 607, 615, 618
16.10	Puma	HX212, ON139, ONS138	224, 301, 383, 436, 441, 443, 563, 602, 606, 621, 624, 753, 757
22.10	Steitaxt	SL125	134, 203, 409, 509, 510, 572, 604, 659
24.10	Veilchen	ON140, SC107	71, 84, 89, 132, 381, 402, 437, 438, 442, 454, 571, 658, 704
01.11	Delphin	Transit to Mediterranean	
01.11	Natter	ON143	92, 98, 224, 384, 436, 564, 566, 606, 613, 624, 753
08.11	Schlagetot	UGF1, Allied landings in North Africa	103, 108, 130, 173, 509, 510, 511, 572, 752
08.11	Westwall	UGS, West of Spain near Gibraltar	86, 91, 92, 98, 103, 106, 130, 155, 185, 218, 263, 411, 413, 432, 515, 519, 564, 613, 618, 653
09.11	Kreuzotter	ONS144 then moved to Gibraltar	84, 184, 224, 262, 384, 454, 521, 522, 606, 611, 624, 753
24.11	Drachen	E. of Newfoundland	262, 445, 454, 522, 611, 623, 663
29.11	Panzer	HX217	135, 211, 254, 439, 465, 524, 758
30.11	Draufgänger	HX217, ONS148	221, 455, 553, 569, 600, 604, 609, 610, 615
09.12	Büffel	HX218	373, 445, 663
11.12	Raubold	HX218, ON153, ONS152	135, 203, 211, 356, 409, 410, 439, 600, 610, 621, 623, 664
13.12	Ungestüm	HX218, ON153, ONS152, ONS154	336, 435, 455, 524, 569, 662, 664
21.12	Spitz	ONS154	123, 203, 225, 260, 356, 406, 440, 659, 662, 664
29.12	Delphin	TM1, GUS2	125, 381, 436, 442, 511, 514, 552, 571, 575, 620
1943			
01.01	Habicht	ONS160	186, 268, 303, 383, 438, 613, 624, 704, 752
08.01	Falke	HX?, ON158	69, 71, 167, 201, 226, 257, 333, 384, 403, 404, 414, 441, 444, 525, 563, 572, 584, 606, 607, 631, 632, 706
11.01	Jaguar	HX222, SC116	96, 123, 266, 337, 413, 594, 598, 662, 706
22.01	Landsknecht	West of Ireland	71, 187, 257, 262, 267, 333, 384, 402, 404, 444, 454, 456, 465, 553, 572, 584, 609, 614, 631, 632

DATE	NAME OF U-BOAT GROUP	AREA/CONVOY ATTACKED	U-BOATS (THE 'U' PREFIX HAS BEEN OMITTED)
1943			
22.01	Haudegen	HX223, HX225, ONS165, SG19, UR59	69, 186, 201, 223, 226, 268, 303, 358, 383, 403, 414, 438, 466, 525, 606, 607, 613, 624, 704, 707, 752
31.01	Rochen	KMS, OG	43, 66, 87, 202, 218, 258, 264, 504, 521, 558
01.02	Pfeil	SC118	89, 135, 187, 262, 266, 267, 402, 413, 454, 465, 594, 608, 609
02.02	Seehund	Off South Africa	160, 182, 506, 509, 516 with supply boats 459 & 117
04.02	Hartherz	KMS, MKS, West of Biscay	71, 107, 183, 332, 519, 572, 584, 621, 628, 653, 753
11.02	Knappen	ON166	91, 92, 600, 604
13.02	Ritter	HX226	225, 332, 377, 454, 468, 529, 603, 623, 628, 653, 753
15.02	Taifun	ONS165	186, 223, 358, 707
16.02	Neptun	HX226, ON166	135, 359, 376, 405, 448, 566, 608, 659, 759
16.02	Robbe	SW of Spain	103, 107, 382, 410, 437, 445, 511, 569
21.02	Sturmbock	ONS167	84, 432, 591, 758
25.02	Wildfang	ON166, ONS176	84, 226, 332, 383, 409, 432, 591, 607, 664, 753, 758
26.02	Burggraf	ON168, ON170, SC121	91, 228, 230, 332, 359, 405, 435, 448, 468, 523, 526, 527, 566, 600, 603, 615, 616, 621, 634, 653, 659, 709
28.02	Tümmler	UGS3, West of Canary Islands	43, 66, 202, 504, 521, 558
06.03	Westmark	SC121	228, 230, 332, 359, 405, 409, 432, 448, 527, 566, 591, 616, 634
06.03	Neuland	HX228	86, 190, 229, 373, 406, 439, 440, 441, 447, 530, 618, 633, 641, 642, 665, 757
07.03	Raubgraf	HX228, HX229, ON168, ON170, ONS169, SC122	84, 89, 91, 435, 468, 600, 603, 615, 621, 638, 653, 664, 758
08.03	Ostmark	SC121	190, 229, 439, 447, 530, 618, 641, 642, 665
10.03	Unversagt	UGS3	106, 130, 167, 172, 513, 515
11.03	Stürmer	HX229, SC122	134, 190, 229, 305, 338, 384, 439, 523, 526, 527, 530, 598, 618, 631, 641, 642, 665, 666
13.03	Wohlgemut	UGS3, near Azores	67, 103, 109, 159, 524
14.03	Dränger	HX229, SC122	86, 221, 333, 373, 406, 440, 590, 608, 610
21.03	Seeteufel	ONS1 (New series after ONS171)	91, 134, 188, 260, 306, 415, 523, 526, 564, 572, 592, 610, 632, 663, 706
22.03	Seeräuber	RS3 near Canaries	67, 123, 159, 167, 172, 513, 515
22.03	Seeteufel	ONS?, HX230	Same boats as in original group
25.03	Seewolf	HX230, SC123 South of Seeteufel	84, 86, 257, 305, 333, 336, 373, 440, 441, 527, 530, 590, 591, 615, 618, 631, 641, 642, 666
29.03	Löwenherz	HX231	168, 191, 260, 563, 564, 572, 584, 592, 594, 630, 632, 635, 706
07.04	Adler	HX232, ON176, SC125	71, 84, 188, 257, 267, 404, 571, 613, 615, 662
11.04	Lerche	HX232, ON176	168, 191, 203, 260, 270, 532, 563, 584, 630, 706
11.04	Meise	HX234	84, 108, 134, 191, 203, 257, 258, 267, 306, 381, 404, 413, 415, 438, 552, 571, 598, 610, 613, 631, 706
14.04	Drossel	HX237, SL128	89, 221, 230, 406, 436, 439, 447, 456, 600, 607, 657, 659, 735
20.04	Specht	HX235	92, 108, 125, 168, 203, 226, 260, 264, 270, 358, 438, 514, 584, 614, 628, 630, 662, 706, 707, 732
26.04	Amsel	ONS5, SC127	107, 223, 266, 377, 383, 402, 504, 575, 621, 634, 638
26.04	Fink	ONS5	107, 402, 504, 575, 621, 628, 638
28.04	Star	ONS5	209, 231, 386, 413, 528, 531, 532, 533, 648, 650
04.05	Star & Specht combined	SC128	125, 168, 192, 209, 226, 231, 260, 264, 270, 358, 378, 381, 413, 438, 514, 531, 533, 552, 584, 614, 628, 630, 632, 648, 650, 662, 707, 732, 954
08.05	Elbe	SC129	103, 107, 186, 223, 231, 267, 359, 377, 383, 402, 448, 454, 466, 468, 504, 514, 525, 569, 575, 584, 621, 634, 650, 709, 752

DATE	NAME OF U-BOAT GROUP	AREA/CONVOY ATTACKED	U-BOATS (THE 'U' PREFIX HAS BEEN OMITTED)
1943			
08.05	Lech	ONS7	91, 202, 209, 664
08.05	Rhein	HX237	103, 186, 359, 403, 448, 454, 466, 468, 525, 569, 709, 752
11.05	Isar	ONS7	304, 418, 645, 952
12.05	Inn	ONS7	92, 258, 381, 954
12.05	Iller	ONS7	340, 636, 657, 731, 760
15.05	Donau	ONS7	91, 92, 202, 209, 218, 258, 264, 304, 340, 378, 381, 413, 418, 645, 657, 664, 686, 707, 731, 760, 952, 954
18.05	Oder	HX238	221, 228, 336, 558, 603, 642, 666, 752
19.05	Mosel	HX239	218, 221, 228, 231, 264, 305, 336, 378, 441, 468, 552, 558, 569, 575, 603, 607, 621, 642, 650, 666, 752
01.06	Trutz	GUS7a, West of Canaries	92, 211, 217, 221, 228, 232, 336, 435, 558, 603, 608, 641, 642, 666, 951, 953
07.06		Simulating strong formation in North Atlantic by radio deception	271, 334, 341, 388, 420, 592, 667, 669
16.06	Eins	GUS8	228, 558, 608, 642
16.06	Zwei	GUS8	135, 232, 336, 603, 641, 666, 951, 953
16.06	Drei	GUS8	193, 211, 221, 435
01.07	Geier	GUS7a, OS51	228, 608, 633, 641
01.07	Geier 2	GUS7a, OS51	211, 435, 951, 953
01.07	Geier 3	GUS7a, OS51	232, 336, 642
17.07	Monsun	Indian Ocean	168, 183, 188, 532, 533
13.09	Leuthen	ON202, ONS8	229, 238, 260, 270, 275, 305, 338, 341, 377, 378, 386, 402, 442, 584, 603, 641, 645, 666, 731, 758, 952
26.09	Rossbach	HX259, ON203, ON204, ONS19, SC143	91, 260, 275, 279, 305, 309, 336, 378, 389, 402, 419, 448, 539, 584, 603, 610, 631, 641, 643, 645, 666, 731, 758, 762, 952
01.10	Monsun	Between Bear Is. and Spitzbergen	269, 277, 307, 355, 360, 387, 713, 737, 956
13.10	Schlieffen	ONS20	91, 231, 267, 271, 413, 426, 437, 448, 540, 668, 762, 841, 842
23.10	Schill	MKS28, MKS29, SL138, W. of Spain	211, 228, 262, 333, 358, 515, 600
23.10	Siegfried	HX262	91, 212, 226, 231, 267, 281, 309, 373, 405, 413, 420, 426, 437, 552, 575,
			592, 608, 648, 709, 762, 842, 963, 967, 969
28.10	Körner	East of Newfoundland	212, 231, 267, 281, 413, 580, 586, 714, 843, 963, 969
31.10	Jahn	East of Newfoundland	226, 379, 426, 437, 552, 575, 608, 648, 709, 842
12.11	Eisenbart	HX264, SC146	212, 280, 282, 343, 391, 424, 538, 542, 552, 575, 586, 648, 709, 714, 764, 843, 963, 967, 969
22.11	Weddingen	MKS31, OG95, SL140	107, 228, 238, 358, 391, 424, 618, 843
04.12	Coronel	HX268, ONS214, ONS215	92, 269, 415, 421, 541, 543, 544, 625, 629, 653, 667, 672, 734, 761, 801, 962
20.12	Borkum	MKS33, MKS34, SL142	107, 228, 238, 358, 391, 424, 618, 843
22.12	Amrum, Föhr, Rügen, Sylt	West of Britain	92, 302, 311, 364, 390, 392, 421, 471, 545, 546, 625, 653, 672, 744, 781, 960, 972, 976, 981
1944			
01.01	Stier	JW63, RA58	293, 299, 310, 636, 956, 995, 997
07.01	Rügen		212, 231, 238, 302, 305, 309, 311, 364, 377, 382, 390, 392, 471, 545, 547, 552, 571, 592, 641, 666, 731, 741, 757, 762, 846, 972, 976, 981
16.01	Isegrim	JW56	278, 314, 360, 425, 601, 716, 737, 739, 957, 965
27.01	Stürmer	KMS40, ON221, OS66	390, 547, 731, 762, 984, 989
31.01	Hinein	KMS40, ON221, OS66	212, 271, 281, 571, 592, 650
31.01	Igel	ON223, ON233, OS66	212, 283, 386, 406, 441, 545, 547, 549, 666, 714, 984, 985, 989

DATE	NAME OF U-BOAT GROUP	AREA/CONVOY ATTACKED	U-BOATS (THE 'U' PREFIX HAS BEEN OMITTED)
1944			
14.02	Hai	ONS, OS33, SW Ireland - W of Africa	91, 212, 231, 256, 264, 281, 386, 406, 424, 437, 441, 546, 549, 603, 608, 650, 709, 764, 963, 985, 989
20.02	Preussen	N of Azores - W of Ireland	91, 212, 256, 262, 281, 358, 437, 441, 448, 603, 608, 709, 764, 962, 963, 985
20.02	Werwolf	JW57, RA57	312, 313, 362, 425, 601, 674, 713, 739, 956, 990
21.02	Hartmut	JW57, RA57	315, 366, 472, 673
28.02	Boreas	Kola Inlet	307, 315, 472, 739
28.02	Hartmut	JW57, RA57	315, 366, 472, 673
22.03	Landwirt	Anti-invasion group, W of France - Training	740, 766, 821, 970, 993
01.04	Thor	Arctic, JW58, RA58	278, 312, 313, 674
01.04	Blitz	Arctic	277, 355, 711, 956
01.04	Hammer	Arctic	288, 315, 354, 968
09.04	Donner Keil	JW58, RA58	277, 313, 347, 361, 362, 636, 703, 711, 716, 990
29.04	Donner	JW58	277, 313, 347, 361, 362, 636, 703, 711, 716, 990
30.04	Keil	JW58	Boats from Donner
30.04	Igel 2	ON233, ONS29	91, 238, 256, 281, 424, 445, 546, 618, 650, 709, 731, 734, 963
20.05	Dragoner	W of Channel	269, 441, 764, 953, 984
08.06	Mitte	Anti-invasion group off Norway	242, 276, 286, 299, 317, 319, 397, 677, 715, 745, 771, 975, 982, 987, 994, 998, 999, 1001, 1007, 1156, 1192
06.08	Greif		278, 362, 365, 711, 739, 957
17.09	Grimm	JW60, RA60	278, 312, 425, 737, 921, 956, 997
27.11	Stock	JW62, RA62	286, 293, 299, 313, 315, 318, 363, 365, 992, 995
27.11	Grube	JW62, RA62	295, 310, 387, 668, 965, 997, 1163
1945			
06.02	Rasmus	JW64	286, 307, 425, 636, 711, 716, 739, 968
14.03	Hagen	JW65	307, 312, 313, 363, 711, 716, 968, 992, 997
17.04	Faust	JW66, PK9	286, 295, 307, 313, 363, 481 later joined by 278, 294, 312, 318, 427, 711, 716, 968, 992, 997

Left: Survivors from the *Breiviken* sunk by U178.

German Officer Ranks and their British Equivalents

GERMAN RANK	COMMON ABBREVIATION	BRITISH EQUIVALENT
Grossadmiral		Admiral of the Fleet
Generaladmiral		No equivalent
Admiral		Admiral
Vizeadmiral		Vice Admiral
Konteradmiral		Rear Admiral
Flotillenadmiral		Commodore
Kapitän zur See	KptzS	Captain
Fregattenkapitän	Fregkpt	No equivalent
Korvettenkapitän	Korvkpt	Commander
Kapitänleutnant	Kptlt	Lieutenant Commander
Oberleutnant zur See	ObltzS	Lieutenant
Leutnant zur See	LtzS	Sub-Lieutenant
Fähnrich zur See		Midshipman

Kommodore was not a rank within the German navy, but an appointment. Therefore the title usually was 'KptzS und Kommodore'.

Above: Although the navy was a stickler for regulations, once at sea U-boat men wore what was most comfortable without regard to the rules, and badges of rank were hardly necessary.

Appendix IV
Essential Wartime Statistics

MONTH	SHIPS SUNK BY U-BOATS	U-BOATS AT SEA	SHIPS SUNK PER U-BOAT AT SEA
September 1939	41	23	1.8
October	27	10	2.7
November	21	16	1.3
December	25	8	3.1
January 1940	40	11	3.6
February	45	15	3.0
March	23	13	1.8
April	7	24	0.3
May	13	8	1.6
June	58	18	3.2
July	38	11	3.5
August	56	13	4.3
September	59	13	4.5
October	63	12	5.3
November	33	11	3.0
December	37	10	3.7
January 1941	21	8	2.6
February	39	12	3.3
March	41	13	3.2
April	43	19	2.3
May	58	24	2.4
June	61	32	1.9
July	22	27	0.8
August	23	36	0.6
September	53	36	1.5
October	32	36	0.9
November	13	38	0.3
December	26	25	1.0
January 1942	62	42	1.5
February	85	50	1.7
March	95	48	2.0
April	74	49	1.5
May	125	61	2.0
June	144	59	2.4
July	96	70	1.4

MONTH	SHIPS SUNK BY U-BOATS	U-BOATS AT SEA	SHIPS SUNK PER U-BOAT AT SEA
August	108	86	1.3
September	98	100	1.0
October	94	105	0.9
November	119	95	1.3
December	60	97	0.6
January 1943	37	92	0.4
February	63	116	0.5
March	108	116	0.9
April	56	111	0.5
May	50	118	0.4
June	20	86	0.2
July	46	84	0.5
August	16	59	0.3
September	20	60	0.3
October	20	86	0.2
November	14	78	0.2
December	13	67	0.2
January 1944	13	66	0.2
February	18	68	0.3
March	23	68	0.3
April	9	57	0.2
May	4	43	0.1
June	11	47	0.2
July	12	34	0.4
August	18	50	0.4
September	7	68	0.1
October	1	45	0.0
November	7	41	0.2
December	9	51	0.2
January 1945	11	39	0.3
February	15	47	0.3
March	13	56	0.2
April	13	54	0.2
May	3	45	0.1

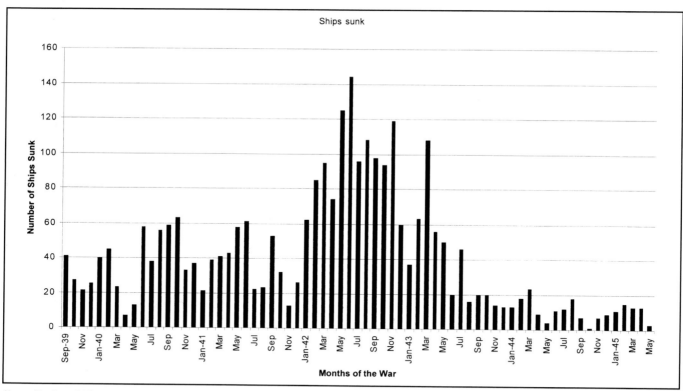

Above: Number of Allied ships sunk per month of the war.

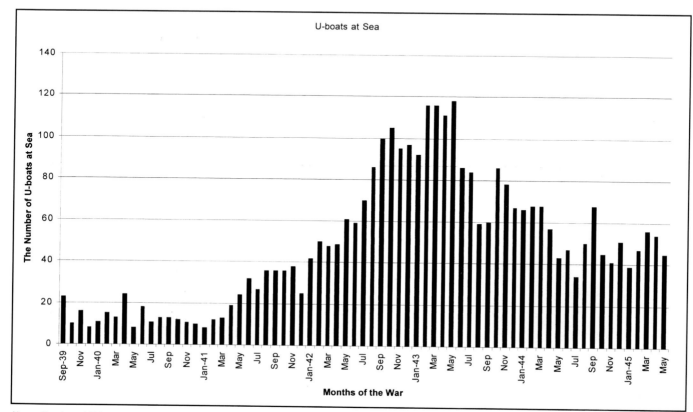

Above: Number of U-boats at sea per month of the war.

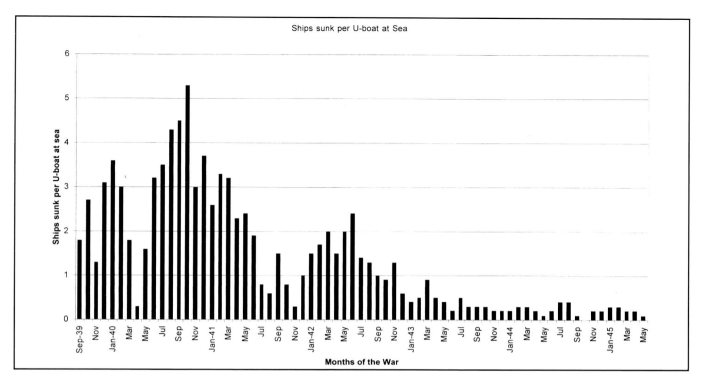

Above: Number of Allied ships sunk per U-boat at sea, per month of the war.

Above: Victims of war.

Further Reading

Banks, Arthur; *Wings of the Dawning*; Images Publishing, Malvern Wells, 1996. (An interesting and well illustrated account of the Battle for the Indian Ocean.)

Beesly, Patrick; *Very Special Intelligence*; Hamish Hamilton, London, 1977 and Doubleday, New York, 1978. (An interesting book dealing with the Operational Intelligence Centre in London by the deputy leader of the Submarine Tracking Room.)

Bonatz, Heinz; *Seekrieg im Äther*; Mittler & Sohn, Herford, 1981.

Brennecke, Jochen; *Jäger–Gejagte*; Koehlers Verlag, Jugendheim, 1956. (One of the early classics with excellent descriptions of life aboard U-boats.)

Brunswick, Hans; *Feuersturm über Hamburg*; Motorbuch Verlag, Stuttgart, 1992. (An excellent book about the terror raids on Hamburg.)

Brustat-Naval, Fritz; *Ali Cremer–U333*; Ullstein, Frankfurt am Main, 1982.
— and Suhren, Teddy; *Nasses Eichenlaub*; Koehlers, Herford, 1983.

Buchheim, Lothar-Günther; *Ubootskrieg*; Piper, Munich, 1976. (Contains a vast number of fascinating photographs taken by the author while serving as war correspondent.)

Busch, Harald; *So war der Ubootskrieg* (*U-boats at War*); Deutsche Heimat Verlag, Bielefeld, 1954. (This early account by an ex-war correspondent has become a classic on this subject.)

Busch, Rainer, and Röll, Hans-Joachim; *Der U-Boot-Krieg 1939 bis 1945. Vol 1, Die deutschen U-Boot-Kommandanten*; Koehler/Mittler, Hamburg, Berlin, Bonn 1996. Published in English by Greenhill as *U-boat Commanders*. (Brief biographies produced from the records of the German U-Boot-Archiv. Sadly the English edition has been published without the numerous corrections recorded by the Archive.)
— *Der U-Boot-Krieg 1939-1945*; E. S. Mittler & Sohn, Hamburg, Berlin and Bonn, 1999 (German U-boat losses from September 1939 to May 1945 from the records of the U-Boot-Archiv.)

Compton-Hall, Richard; *The Underwater War 1939-45*; Blandford Press, Poole, 1982 (The author was the Director of the Royal Navy's Submarine Museum and this is by far the best book for describing life in submarines.)

Cremer, Peter; *U-boat Commander*; The Bodley Head, London, 1982.

Dollinger, Hans; *The Decline and Fall of Nazi Germany and Imperial Japan*; Odhams, London, 1965. (Powerful photographic images.)

Dönitz, Karl; *Ten Years and Twenty Days*; Weidenfeld and Nicolson, London, 1959.

— *Mein wechselvolles Leben*; Musterschmidt Verlag, Frankfurt, 1968.

Frank, Dr Wolfgang; *Die Wölfe und der Admiral*; Gerhard Stalling Verlag, Oldenburg, 1953. Translated as *Sea Wolves — The Story of the German U-boat War*; Weidenfeld, London, 1955. (An excellent classic written by a war correspondent who served aboard U-boats.)
— *Prien greift an*; Hans Köhler Verlag, Hamburg, 1942.

Gannon, Michael; *Operation Drumbeat*; Harper and Row, New York, 1990. (An interesting account of the dramatic story of Germany's first U-boat attacks along the American coast.)
— *Black May*; New York, 1998.

Giese, Otto and Wise, Capt James E.; *Shooting the War*; Naval Institute Press, Annapolis, 1994. (A fascinating book. Giese ran the blockade aboard the merchant ship *Anneliese Essberger* and then joined the U-boat Arm to serve in the Arctic, Atlantic and Far East.)

Gretton, Sir Peter; *Crisis Convoy*; Purnell, London, 1974. (The story of convoy HX231, the convoy which crossed the Atlantic in April 1943 and threw off every attacking U-boat.)
— *Convoy Escort Commander*; Cassell, London, 1964.

Gröner, Erich; *Die deutschen Kriegsschiffe 1815-1945*; J. F. Lehmanns, Munich, 1968. (This is the standard book giving the technical data of German warships. Much of the information is tabulated, making it relatively easy for non-German readers. However, the section dealing with U-boat losses contains a good proportion of questionable information.)
— *Die Handelsflotten der Welt 1942*; J. F. Lehmanns, Munich, reprinted 1976. (Includes details of ships sunk up to 1942. This valuable publication was originally a confidential document and contains a complete list of ships, in similar style to Lloyd's Register. There is also a lengthy section with good line drawings.)

Hadley, Michael L.; *U-boats against Canada*; McGill-Queen's University Press, Kingston and Montreal, 1985 (An excellent book with detailed information about U-boats which approached the Canadian coast.)
— *Count not the Dead*; McGill-Queen's University Press, Montreal, Kingston and London, 1995.

Hague, Arnold; *The Allied Convoy System 1939-1945*; Vanwell, Ontario and Chatham Publishing, Rochester, 2000.

Harbon, John D.; *The Longest Battle* (*The RCN in the Atlantic 1939-1945*); Vanwell, Ontario, 1993.

Hering, Robert; *Chronik der Crew 37A 1937-1987*; Selbstverlag, Gärtringen, 1987. (An excellent account about officers who joined the navy in 1937.)

Herzog, Bodo; 60 *Jahre deutsche Uboote 1906-1966*; J. F. Lehmanns, Munich, 1968. (A useful book with much tabulated information.)
— *U-boats in Action*; Ian Allan Publishing, Shepperton, 1971 and Podzun, Dorheim. (A pictorial book with captions in English.)

Hessler, Günter, Hoschatt, Alfred and others; *The U-boat War in the Atlantic*; HMSO, 1989.

Hirschfeld, Wolfgang; *Feindfahrten*; Neff, Vienna, 1982. (The secret diary of a U-boat radio operator compiled in the radio rooms of operational submarines. A most invaluable insight into the war and probably one of the most significant accounts of the war at sea.)
— *Das Letzte Boot — Atlantik Farewell*; Universitas, Munich, 1989. (The last journey of *U234*, surrender in the United States and life as a prisoner of war.)
— and Geoffrey Brooks; *Hirschfeld — The Story of a U-boat NCO 1940-46*; Leo Cooper, London, 1996. (A fascinating English language edition of Hirschfeld's life in U-boats.)

Hoffmann, Rudolf; *50 Jahre Olympia-Crew*; Selbstverlag, Hamburg, 1986 and 88. (An excellent account about the men who joined the navy in 1936.)

Högel, Georg; *Embleme Wappen Malings deutscher Uboote 1939-1945*; Koehlers, Hamburg, Berlin, Bonn, 1997. Published in English as *U-boat Emblems of World War II 1939-1945*; Schiffer Military History, Atglen, 1999. (An excellent work dealing with U-boat emblems, especially those which were painted on conning towers. Very well illustrated with drawings by the author who served as radio operator in *U30* and *U110*.)

Jones, Geoff; *The Month of the Lost U-boats*; William Kimber, London, 1977.
— *Autumn of the U-boats*; William Kimber, London, 1984. (About the autumn of 1943.)
— *U-boat Aces*; William Kimber, London, 1984.
— *Defeat of the Wolf Packs*; William Kimber, London, 1986.
— *Submarines versus U-boats*; William Kimber, London, 1986.

Jung, D., Maass, M. and Wenzel, B.; *Tanker und Versorger der deutschen Flotte 1900-1980*; Motorbuch, Stuttgart, 1981. (This excellent book is the standard reference work on the German supply system.)

Kemp, Paul; *U-boats Destroyed*; Arms and Armour, London, 1997. (Some of this book has been superseded by more up-to-date information, but the explanations for each boat are comprehensive and it is an easy-to-use reference book.)

Kohnen, David; *Commanders Winn and Knowles: Winning the U-boat War with Intelligence 1939-1943*; The Enigma Press, Krakow, 1999. (An interesting book, although the name Rodger Winn is misspellt as Roger throughout.)

Koop, Gerhard and Mulitze, Erich; *Die Marine in Wilhelmshaven*; Bernard & Graefe Verlag, Koblenz, 1987. (Well illustrated and should also appeal to readers with only a small knowledge of German.)

— and Galle, K. and Klein F.; *Von der Kaiserlichen Werft zum Marinearsenal*; Bernard & Graefe Verlag, Munich, 1982. (A fascinating and well-illustrated history of the naval base in Wilhelmshaven.)

Lohmann, W. and Hildebrand, H. H.; *Die deutsche Kriegsmarine 1939-1945*; Podzun, Dorheim, 1956-1964. (This multi-volume work is the standard reference document on the German navy, giving details of ships, organisation and personnel.)

Lüth, Wolfgang and Korth, Claus; *Boot greift wieder an!*; Erich Klinghammer, Berlin, 1943.

Macintyre, Donald; *The Battle of the Atlantic*; Batsford, London, 1971.

McKee, Fraser and Darlington, Robert; *The Canadian Naval Chronicles 1939-1945*; Vanwell, St Catherines, 1996.

Merten, Karl-Friedrich and Baberg, Kurt; *Wir Ubootfahrer sagen 'Nein — So war das nicht'*; J. Reiss Verlag, Grossaitingen, 1986.

Metzler, Jost; *The Laughing Cow*; William Kimber, London, 1955.

Milner, Marc; *North Atlantic Run*; Naval Institute Press, Annapolis, 1985.

Möller, Eberhard; *Kurs Atlantik*; Motorbuch Verlag, Stuttgart, 1995

Moore, Captain Arthur R.; *A careless word . . . a needless sinking*; American Merchant Marine Museum, Maine, 1983. (A detailed and well-illustrated account of ships lost during the war.)

Mulligan, Timothy P.; *Neither Sharks Nor Wolves*; United States Naval Institute Press, Annapolis, 1999 and Chatham Publishing, London, 1999. (An excellent book about the men who manned the U-boats.)
— *Lone Wolf*; Praeger, Westport & London, 1993. (An excellent account about the life and death of the U-boat ace Werner Henke of *U515*.)

Nesbit, Roy Conyers; *RAF Coastal Command in Action 1939-1945*; Sutton, Stroud, 1997. (Excellent photographs, from the 'In Camera' series.)

Niestle, Axel; *German U-boat Losses during World War II*; Greenhill, London, 1998. (Well researched with up-to-date basic information, but lacking explanations and badly laid out, making it difficult to use as a reference book.)

OKM (Supreme Naval Command); *Bekleidungs und Anzugsbestimmungen für die Kriegsmarine*; Berlin, 1935; reprinted Jak P. Mallmann Showell, 1979. (The official dress regulations of the German navy.)
— *Rangliste der deutschen Kriegsmarine*; Mittler & Sohn, published annually, Berlin.

— *Handbuch für U-boot-Kommandanten*; Berlin, 1942. Translated during the war and published by Thomas Publications, Gettysburg, 1989 as *The U-boat Commander's Handbook.*

Plottke, Herbert; *Fächer Loos! (U172 in Einsatz)*; Podzun-Pallas, Wölfersheim-Berstadt, 1997.

Poolman, Kenneth; *The Catafighters*; William Kimber, London, 1970.

Preston, Anthony; *U-boats*; Bison Books, London, 1978. (Well illustrated with good photographs.)

Prien, Günther; *U-boat Commander*; Tempus Publishing, Stroud, 2000. (A reprint of this well-known book by the commander of *U47*, although some of the comments must be taken with a great pinch of salt and were probably not written by Prien.)

Raeder, Erich; *Struggle for the Sea*; William Kimber, London, 1966.
— *My Life*; US Naval Institute Press, 1960.

Reintjes, Karl Heinrich; *U524 — Das Kriegstagebuch eines U-bootes*; Ernst Knoth, Melle, 1994. (A well-annotated copy of the boat's log book.)

Robertson, Terrence; *The Golden Horseshoe*; Tempus Publishing, Stroud, 2000. (A reprint of this early classic about *U99* and Otto Kretschmer.)

Rohde, Jens; *Die Spur des Löwen — U1202*; Libri Books on Demand, Itzehoe, 2000. (Most of this interesting book contains pictures and facsimiles, meaning it is not too difficult for people with only a smattering of German.)

Rohwer, J.; *Axis Submarine Successes of World War II 1939-45*; Greenhill, London, 1998.
— *Uboote: Eine Chronik in Bildern*; Gerhard Stalling Verlag, Oldenburg, 1962.
— *The Critical Convoy Battles of March 1943*; Ian Allan Publishing, London, 1977.
and Hümmelchen, G.; *Chronology of the War at Sea 1939-1945*; Greenhill, London, 1992. (A good, solid and informative work. Well indexed and extremely useful for anyone studying the war at sea.)
and Jacobsen, H. A.; *Decisive Battles of World War II*; André Deutsch, London, 1965.

Roskill, Captain S. W.; *The War at Sea*; 4 vols, HMSO, London, 1954, reprinted 1976. (The official history of the war at sea.)

Rössler, Eberhard; *Die deutschen Uboote und ihre Werften*; Bernard & Graefe, Koblenz, 1979.
— *Geschichte des deutschen Ubootbaus*; Bernard & Graefe, Koblenz, 1986.
— *The U-boat*; Arms and Armour Press, London, 1981.

Sarty, Roger; *Canada and the Battle of the Atlantic*; Art Global, Montreal, 1998.

Schaeffer, Heinz; *U-boat 977*; William Kimber, London, 1952.

Schenk, Robert; *What it was like to be a sailor in World War II*; Naval Institute Press, Annapolis

Schlemm, Jürgen; *Der U-Boot-Krieg 1939-1945 in der Literatur*; Elbe-Spree-Verlag, Hamburg and Berlin, 2000. (A comprehensive bibliography of publications about the U-boat war.)

Schoenfeld, Max; *Stalking the U-boat*; Smithsonian Institution Press, Washington and London, 1995. (An interesting account of the USAAF anti-submarine operations.)

Schulz, Wilhelm; *Über dem nassen Abgrund*; E. S. Mittler & Sohn, Berlin, Bonn and Herford, 1994. (The story of *U124* by one of her commanders.)

Seeger, Hans; *Militärische Ferngläser und Fernrohre in Heer, Luftwaffe und Marine* (*Military Binoculars and Telescopes for Land, Air and Sea Service*); Dr Hans T. Seeger, Hamburg 1995. (An excellent volume with two key chapters and photographic captions in English.)
— *Optisches Gerät der deutschen Wehrtechnik* (German Military Technology: Optical Equipment); Dr Hans T. Seeger, Hamburg, 1997. (Dealing with descriptive documents circulated by Carl Zeiss, Jena, between 1930 and 1940.)

Sharpe, Peter; *U-boat Fact File*; Midland Publishing, Leicester, 1998. (A handy reference book, well laid out and easy to use.)

Showell, Jak P. Mallmann; *The German Navy in World War Two*; Arms and Armour Press, London, 1979; Naval Institute Press, Annapolis 1979 and translated as *Das Buch der deutschen Kriegsmarine*, Motorbuch Verlag, Stuttgart, 1982. (Covers history, organisation, the ships, code writers, naval charts and a section on ranks, uniforms, awards and insignias by Gordon Williamson. Named by the United States Naval Institute as 'One of the Outstanding Naval Books of the Year'.)
— *U-boats under the Swastika*; Ian Allan Publishing, Shepperton, 1973; Arco, New York, 1973 and translated as *Uboote gegen England*, Motorbuch, Stuttgart, 1974. (A well-illustrated introduction to the German U-boat Arm, and now one of the longest-selling naval books in Germany.)
— *U-boats under the Swastika*; Ian Allan Publishing, Shepperton, 1987. (A second edition with different photos and new text of the above title.)
— *U-boat Command and the Battle of the Atlantic*; Conway Maritime Press, London, 1989; Vanwell, New York, 1989. (A detailed history based on the U-boat Command's war diary.)
— 'Germania International'; *Journal of the German Navy Study Group*. Now out of print.
— *U-boat Commanders and Crews*; The Crowood Press, Marlborough, 1998. Translated as: *Die U-Boot-Waffe: Kommandanten und Besatzungen*; Motorbuch Verlag, Stuttgart, 2001.
— *German Navy Handbook 1939-1945*; Sutton Publishing, Stroud, 1999. Translated as: *Kriegsmarine 1939-1945*; Motorbuch Verlag, Stuttgart, 2000.
— *U-boats in Camera 1939-1945*; Sutton Publishing, Stroud, 1999.
— *Enigma U-boats*; Ian Allan Publishing; Shepperton 2000.

— *U-boats at War — Landings on Hostile Shores*; Ian Allan Publishing, Shepperton, 2000.
— *Hitler's U-boat Bases*; Sutton Publishing, Stroud, 2001.
— *What Britain knew and Wanted to Know about U-boats*, selected, annotated reprints from the secret Monthly Anti-Submarine Reports; published for U-Boot-Archiv by Military Press, Milton Keynes, 2001.

Slader, John; *The Red Duster at War*; William Kimber, London, 1988.

Smith, Constance Babington; *Evidence in Camera*; David Charles, Newton Abbot, 1957 and 1974. (An interesting book about British aerial photo-reconnaissance.)

Spooner, A.; *In Full Flight*; Macdonald, London, 1965. (Interesting account on how Coastal Command attacked U-boats.)

Tennent, Alan J.; *British and Commonwealth Merchant Ship Losses to Axis Submarines 1939-1945*; Sutton Publishing, Stroud, 2001.

Topp, Erich; *Fackeln über dem Atlantik*; Ullstein, Berlin, 1999. (the autobiography of a famous U-boat commander.)

U-Boot-Archiv; *Das Archiv* (German) — *The U-boat Archive* (English language); a journal published twice a year for members of FTU, U-Boot-Archiv, Bahnhofstrasse 57, D-27478 Cuxhaven-Altenbruch. (Please enclose at least two International Postal Reply Coupons if asking for details.)

Verband Deutscher Ubootsfahrer; *Schaltung Küste* (Journal of the German Submariners' Association)

Wagner, Gerhard (editor); *Lagevorträge des Oberbefehlshabers der Kriegsmarine vor Hitler*; J. F. Lehmanns, Munich, 1972. Translated as *Fuehrer Conferences on Naval Affairs*, Greenhill, London, reprinted with new introduction, 1990. (The first English language edition was published before the German version.)

Waters, Captain J. M. Jn.; *Bloody Winter*; D. van Nostrand, 1967.

White, John F.; *U-boat Tankers 1941-45*; Airlife Publishing, Shrewsbury, 1998.

Williamson, Gordon; *The Iron Cross*; Blandford Press, Poole, 1986.
— *The Knight's Cross of the Iron Cross*; Blandford Press, Poole, 1987.
and Pavlovik, Darko; *U-boat Crews 1914-45*; Osprey, London, 1995. (An interesting book with excellent colour drawings and black and white photographs.)
— *Grey Wolf*; Osprey, London, 2001.
— *German Seaman 1939-45*; Osprey, London, 2001.

Witthöft, Hans Jürgen; *Lexikon zur deutschen Marinegeschichte*; Koehler, Herford, 1977. (An excellent two-volume encyclopaedia.)

Wynn, Kenneth; *U-boat Operations of World War 2*; Chatham, London, 1997.

Y'Blood, William T.; *Hunter – Killer: U.S. Escort Carriers in the Battle of the Atlantic*; Naval Institute Press, Annapolis, 1983.

Zienert, J.; *Unsere Marineuniform*; Helmut Gerhard Schulz, Hamburg, 1970. (The standard work on German naval uniforms.)

Left: OL H. Winkesdorf and (right) Matgfr Vehing photographed whilst serving on U673.

Index